INTERNATIONAL WILDLIFE TRAFFICKING THREATS TO CONSERVATION AND NATIONAL SECURITY

HEARING

BEFORE THE

COMMITTEE ON FOREIGN AFFAIRS
HOUSE OF REPRESENTATIVES

ONE HUNDRED THIRTEENTH CONGRESS

SECOND SESSION

FEBRUARY 26, 2014

Serial No. 113–143

Printed for the use of the Committee on Foreign Affairs

Available via the World Wide Web: http://www.foreignaffairs.house.gov/ or
http://www.gpo.gov/fdsys/

U.S. GOVERNMENT PRINTING OFFICE

86–869PDF   WASHINGTON : 2014

For sale by the Superintendent of Documents, U.S. Government Printing Office
Internet: bookstore.gpo.gov   Phone: toll free (866) 512–1800; DC area (202) 512–1800
Fax: (202) 512–2104   Mail: Stop IDCC, Washington, DC 20402–0001

COMMITTEE ON FOREIGN AFFAIRS

EDWARD R. ROYCE, California, *Chairman*

CHRISTOPHER H. SMITH, New Jersey
ILEANA ROS-LEHTINEN, Florida
DANA ROHRABACHER, California
STEVE CHABOT, Ohio
JOE WILSON, South Carolina
MICHAEL T. McCAUL, Texas
TED POE, Texas
MATT SALMON, Arizona
TOM MARINO, Pennsylvania
JEFF DUNCAN, South Carolina
ADAM KINZINGER, Illinois
MO BROOKS, Alabama
TOM COTTON, Arkansas
PAUL COOK, California
GEORGE HOLDING, North Carolina
RANDY K. WEBER SR., Texas
SCOTT PERRY, Pennsylvania
STEVE STOCKMAN, Texas
RON DeSANTIS, Florida
DOUG COLLINS, Georgia
MARK MEADOWS, North Carolina
TED S. YOHO, Florida
LUKE MESSER, Indiana

ELIOT L. ENGEL, New York
ENI F.H. FALEOMAVAEGA, American
  Samoa
BRAD SHERMAN, California
GREGORY W. MEEKS, New York
ALBIO SIRES, New Jersey
GERALD E. CONNOLLY, Virginia
THEODORE E. DEUTCH, Florida
BRIAN HIGGINS, New York
KAREN BASS, California
WILLIAM KEATING, Massachusetts
DAVID CICILLINE, Rhode Island
ALAN GRAYSON, Florida
JUAN VARGAS, California
BRADLEY S. SCHNEIDER, Illinois
JOSEPH P. KENNEDY III, Massachusetts
AMI BERA, California
ALAN S. LOWENTHAL, California
GRACE MENG, New York
LOIS FRANKEL, Florida
TULSI GABBARD, Hawaii
JOAQUIN CASTRO, Texas

AMY PORTER, *Chief of Staff*   THOMAS SHEEHY, *Staff Director*
JASON STEINBAUM, *Democratic Staff Director*

(II)

CONTENTS

Page

WITNESSES

The Honorable Kerri-Ann Jones, Assistant Secretary, Bureau of Oceans and International Environmental and Scientific Affairs, U.S. Department of State 5

The Honorable Daniel M. Ashe, Director, U.S. Fish and Wildlife Service, U.S. Department of the Interior 17

Mr. Robert G. Dreher, Acting Assistant Attorney General, Environment and Natural Resources Division, U.S. Department of Justice 28

LETTERS, STATEMENTS, ETC., SUBMITTED FOR THE HEARING

The Honorable Kerri-Ann Jones: Prepared statement 8
The Honorable Daniel M. Ashe: Prepared statement 19
Mr. Robert G. Dreher: Prepared statement 30

APPENDIX

Hearing notice...60
Hearing minutes..61
The Honorable Edward R. Royce, a Representative in Congress from the State of California, and chairman, Committee on Foreign Affairs: Material submitted for the record by the National Rifle Association 63
The Honorable Eliot L. Engel, a Representative in Congress from the State of New York: Prepared statement...66
The Honorable Edward R. Royce: Questions submitted for the record to the Honorable Daniel M. Ashe 68
The Honorable Jeff Duncan, a Representative in Congress from the State of South Carolina: Questions submitted for the record to the Honorable Kerri-Ann Jones, the Honorable Daniel M. Ashe and Mr. Robert G. Dreher 71

INTERNATIONAL WILDLIFE TRAFFICKING THREATS TO CONSERVATION AND NATIONAL SECURITY

WEDNESDAY, FEBRUARY 26, 2014

House of Representatives,
Committee on Foreign Affairs,
Washington, DC.

The committee met, pursuant to notice, at 10:11 a.m., in room 2172 Rayburn House Office Building, Hon. Edward Royce (chairman of the committee) presiding.

Chairman ROYCE. This hearing will come to order and I'm going to ask the members to come down to the committee and take their seats so we can get started.

This hearing is on international wildlife trafficking and threats to conservation, threats to security, and I would just start with the observation that we have a major slaughter going on across the African subcontinent.

If we had looked at the numbers a few years ago we would have found that between 1990 and 2005, South Africa lost 14 rhinos a year. Friends, last year there were thousands slaughtered in South Africa.

It gives you a sense of the magnitude of what is happening to the white rhino, the black rhino. If we look at elephants, last year—well, back in 2011, 17,000 elephants were killed in sub-Saharan Africa illegally. Now we go to the following year—30,000 killed in 1 year.

How can this be? How can this new battlefield in this fight end up in such absolute slaughter, threatening the extinction of some of these species?

There is a battlefield there and part of it is with organized crime and part of it is that organized crime has tools that poachers in the past did not have, and increasingly rebel groups and especially terrorist organizations like al-Shabaab are carrying into the fight a new type of weaponry that these animals have not been up against in the past and the battle where this is being carried out is in South Africa's national parks.

Some years ago, some of us worked to set up a national park system—Congo Basin Forest Partnership Act. Well, now those parks across Africa are the battlefield in which these species are being slaughtered.

So as one witness will tell the committee, we are at a pivotal moment in the conservation movement with an alarming and unprecedented dramatic increase in the slaughter of wildlife.

(1)

Driving that slaughter, of course, is the value and we—I talked a little bit here about what happened to the black rhino. The value of rhino horn right now is $60,000 per kilo.

Now, that is more than platinum. That is more than cocaine. So you can see why these criminal syndicates are part of the chain. You can have terrorists or poachers or some of these rebel groups that do the work on the ground but they pass it off to a criminal syndicate that then moves it to market.

If you looked at the cost of ivory, tusk, $1,000 per kilogram. So that makes trafficking among the most lucrative criminal activities worldwide right now, generating $8 billion to $10 billion per year and that cash flow allows today's poacher to buy something he hasn't had in the past. He has got at his disposal helicopters, high-powered weapons, night-vision goggles.

And then you take into account the intelligence community and what they are briefing us on and they are saying that traffickers' use of sophisticated networks is now part of the program to move these products and that this is not just a threat to wildlife anymore.

Increasingly, they say, you have terrorist and rebel groups capitalizing on this trade and that that is a threat to national security.

One example, al-Shabaab—al-Qaeda's affiliate in Somalia—they have turned to the ivory trade for funding. Joseph Kony and his Lord's Resistance Army, when we talked a little bit in the past in these hearings about exploiting child soldiers, well, they are exploiting the region's most unique and limited natural resource to fund its brutal violence as well as exploiting children.

In response to this crisis, I authored legislation last Congress to expand the State Department's rewards program to target transnational criminal syndicates. That has been done.

The first issue—the first example of this is the Pablo Escobar of wildlife trafficking, Vixay Keosavang, has been caught. His number-two man was caught in South Africa and just got 40 years. Ivory and rhino horn were among what was being shipped out of the country.

In order to take a comprehensive look at this—at this problem, the President established an interagency task force. As a starting point the group developed and published the National Strategy for Combating Wildlife Trafficking and we are going to assess that today.

We are going to look forward to hearing that report and, uniquely, the task force also sought advice from an advisory council of outside experts and this included David Barron of the International Conservation Caucus Foundation.

David has worked with Congress for years on these critical issues. There are many others including Africans whose views must be heard on this subject and as this strategy was being developed several of us urged the administration to act boldly to utilize the tools—the law enforcement tools right now that we currently use to dismantle other illicit transnational networks.

I know of no reason why we can't make the same argument, and one thing is clear to me. Whether dealing with global terrorist networks such as Hezbollah or international arms dealers such as Viktor Bout or even—or even tackling North Korea's illicit activities, when the U.S. Government is focused, when the government is directed, it can deliver devastating blows to our enemies.

We have seen that. We have seen them put people like Viktor Bout behind bars. What is needed here is exactly that approach and what we want to do is encourage the administration to do precisely that, and I am sure our NGO groups want to see the same follow through.

So future generations will judge our response to this crisis. If we want a world still blessed with these magnificent species, we need creative action. We need very aggressive action.

We need to work with source and transit and demand to confront the challenge, and as Director Ashe will testify, the criminals have raised their game. We now must do the same, and I will now turn to the ranking member for her opening comment, Karen Bass from Los Angeles.

Ms. BASS. Mr. Chairman, thank you very much for today's hearing and in general for your leadership on this issue.

I know that many people here are aware of Mr. Royce's leadership on this issue for many years but a few months ago I was attending a dinner and had an opportunity to hear his full history on this issue. So I want to thank you for your leadership over many, many years.

I also want to thank our witnesses today for your great work and commitment to solving this international crisis. I am encouraged by the worldwide movement and the administration's focus on this issue and I look forward to continue to be involved in the implementation of the National Strategy for Combating Wildlife Trafficking.

As I know we will hear more of and have heard some, international wildlife trafficking is not only a security and conservation issue but it also undermines the stability and development of many African nations.

Throughout the continent, recent spikes in poaching has caused instability by providing funds for illicit activities, spreading violence and hurting the nation's ability to develop indigenous and local sources of revenue through wildlife tourism.

I have seen first-hand the importance of wildlife tourism to local community development. A couple of years ago, I was on a CODEL to Gabon and also to Botswana and I met with members of communities alongside eco-oriented wildlife sites.

Many of the people provided services for or worked at these eco-sites. In Botswana, for example, I visited a village where the villagers had a contract with a firm in South Africa and the South African company came and helped them develop a small but a high-end resort—tourism resort.

And they were able to, one, employ all of the members of the village in terms of building the resort but also people who came and visited the resort after a few years, they were able to generate $½ million in revenue for the village, which they then plowed back into the development of the village, and it gave me a whole new way to look at this issue.

I know that if trafficking continues at the current rate it will undercut success that has been made at this site and many others and prevent other communities from developing their own strategies to use wildlife tourism and community development.

So I look forward to your testimony today and also to see more of what we can do to end this but also to assist the various nations in their further development.

Thank you very much.

Chairman ROYCE. Thank you, Congresswoman Bass.

Any other members want to make an opening statement? Yes, Mr. Rohrabacher.

Mr. ROHRABACHER. I would like to thank the chairman for holding this hearing, and for those of you who don't know it takes someone to make a decision on how we are going to allocate our time here.

And I think your decision, Mr. Chairman, to hold a hearing on this subject demonstrates the scope as well as the depth of your world view.

And not all chairmen would have a hearing on this issue, and today we acknowledge the destruction of these majestic species in Africa and we realize and we underscore that closing our eyes to this perhaps historic malady that we are facing in humankind today not only is it just the obliteration of wild species in Africa but also as important to our own security, which so often happens when we close our eyes to some evil that is going on. We end up not being able to close our eyes.

As the chairman has pointed out, terrorists and others now are using this very vehicle to handle their own affairs—to pay for their own affairs, which threaten the rest of the world and threaten all of us.

So thank you very much, Mr. Chairman, for your leadership.

Chairman ROYCE. Thank you, Mr. Rohrabacher.

We will go to Mr. Cicilline from Rhode Island.

Mr. CICILLINE. Thank you, Mr. Chairman, and I thank the witnesses for being here today.

Mr. Chairman, I want to just take a moment to applaud your leadership on this issue and to say that I was at the same dinner and I was profoundly moved learning of your very long history in this area.

And I am particularly delighted to also recognize the new but equally passionate leadership of our ranking member of the Africa Subcommittee, Congresswoman Bass, and look forward to what we can do as a committee and as a Congress to address this very important issue, and I thank the witnesses for being here and I yield back.

Chairman ROYCE. Thank you, Mr. Cicilline.

This morning, we are pleased to be joined by representatives from the Department of State, the Department of Interior and the Department of Justice, who represent the three co-chairs of the Presidential Task Force on Wildlife Trafficking.

Prior to her appointment as Assistant Secretary of State for Oceans and International Environment, Dr. Kerri-Ann Jones worked in several capacities within the U.S. Government including positions in the White House Office of Science and Technology Policy, the National Science Foundation, the U.S. Agency for International Development and NIH.

Dr. Daniel Ashe serves as the 16th Director of the U.S. Fish and Wildlife Service, the nation's principal Federal agency dedicated to the conservation of fish and wildlife and the conservation of their habitats.

Earlier in his career, Mr. Ashe was a staffer here on Capitol Hill where he worked, of course, on conservation issues, and welcome back.

As Acting Assistant Attorney General for the Environmental and Natural Resources Division, Mr. Robert Dreher is tasked with prosecuting these environmental crimes, and without objection your full testimony will be put in the record, and if I might suggest you might want to summarize.

If you could hold it to 5 minutes, and members are going to have 5 days to submit any additional statements or questions that you might respond to and any extraneous materials for the record that they might want to put into the record.

So, Dr. Jones, if you could start. We appreciate you being with us.

STATEMENT OF THE HONORABLE KERRI-ANN JONES, ASSISTANT SECRETARY, BUREAU OF OCEANS AND INTERNATIONAL ENVIRONMENTAL AND SCIENTIFIC AFFAIRS, U.S. DEPARTMENT OF STATE

Ms. JONES. Thank you. Good morning, Chairman Royce and Ranking Member Bass, and members of the committee.

I appreciate the opportunity to be here before you today with my colleagues to address wildlife—the wildlife trafficking crisis.

At the outset, I would like to extend my thanks to Chairman Royce and other Members of Congress for focusing strong attention and action on this pernicious multifaceted crisis.

If this is left unchecked, we will be facing more serious threats to conservation, local economies, security as well as health. This terrible problem has been recognized by Congress, by the NGO community around the world, by the private sector and across the executive branch.

The President's July 2013 Executive order called for action, establishing an interagency task force and an advisory council, and earlier this month, as you mentioned, Chairman, the President released the National Strategy for Combating Wildlife Trafficking which lays out a clear whole of government plan forward with three strategic priorities.

These are strengthening domestic and global enforcement, reducing demand for illegally-traded wildlife at home and abroad and building international cooperation and public-private partnerships to combat illegal wildlife poaching and trade.

The September 2013 white paper on wildlife poaching from the Office of the Director of National Intelligence points out that the increasing demand and high profitability of illegal wildlife products has broadened the scope and scale of the problem, particularly in Africa.

African countries are facing mounting security challenges where they are often outgunned by heavily-armed criminal operations. Strengthening enforcement is a necessity and we have taken some actions to begin to address this crisis.

This past November, Secretary Kerry announced the first ever reward for information leading to the dismantling of the Xaysavang Network, a transnational crime syndicate facilitating wildlife trafficking across Africa and Asia.

Chairman Royce's efforts were instrumental in being able to put out this announcement for reward and we thank you, Chairman.

For the last decade, the department has partnered with other U.S. agencies to stand up five regional wildlife enforcement networks and our goal is to connect these regional networks and create a global network.

Our foreign assistance will continue to strengthen policies and legislative frameworks to enhance investigative and law enforcement functions and to support regional cooperation among enforcement agencies.

They will also work to develop capacities to prosecute and adjudicate crimes related to wildlife trafficking. However, to address wildlife trafficking we must also address demand.

We must remove—reduce the market for these products. To do this, we intend to strengthen our efforts with international partners to communicate the negative impacts of this devastating trade on security, environment, local economies and public health.

For example, USAID's Asia Regional Response to Endangered Species Trafficking, or ARREST—the ARREST Project—has launched a series of demand reduction campaigns in Asia's three biggest wildlife market and transit countries and a first Asia-wide smart phone application that will help counter illegal trade in wildlife. And, of course, we will continue to work through our missions around the world to get the message out every way we can.

The third strategic priority recognizes that solutions to this challenging problem require partnerships. We continue to strengthen our diplomatic work to raise the profile of this issue.

We are highlighting the issue in the G–8, in Asia regional bodies and at the U.N. Commission on Crime Prevention and Criminal Justice.

We have secured the inclusion of language to address wildlife trafficking in two security resolutions adopted in January 2014 sanctioning African armed groups.

At the recent London conference, 42 nations in the EU signed on to a declaration that the U.S. helped shape that includes the commitment to avoid the use of endangered species in government purchases and also calls for the continuation of the prohibition of a ban on ivory trade.

We are working with key partners like Indonesia, where just a couple of weeks ago Secretary Kerry signed an MOU with—a memorandum of understanding with Forest Minister Hassan that addresses wildlife and conservation.

We are working with China. Law enforcement entities in China and the U.S. joined other countries including 26 African and Asian nations in a successful global investigative effort, Operation Cobra II.

This was a follow-on to an earlier activity, Cobra I. Both have been very successful. Also, in the upcoming strategic and economic dialogue with China we plan to again address wildlife trafficking and to push for concrete actions in terms of raising public awareness to reduce demand and strengthening law enforcement.

Mr. Chairman, I would like to reiterate Secretary Kerry's continued commitment to tackling this very important illegal trade issue.

We are committed to do more and work smarter with partners around the world to support wildlife range states, to maintain the integrity of their national borders and to protect their iconic wildlife for future generations.

Congress has shown great leadership on this issue. We appreciate your support and we very much look forward to working with you—continuing to work with you on this important issue.

Thank you for the invitation to be here today and I look forward to your questions. Thank you.

[The prepared statement of Ms. Jones follows:]

Statement of
Dr. Kerri-Ann Jones
Assistant Secretary of State
Bureau of Oceans and International Environmental and
Scientific Affairs
U.S. Department of State

Before the Committee on Foreign Affairs
U.S. House of Representatives

February 26, 2014

Introduction

Good morning Chairman Royce, Ranking Member Engel and other Members of the Committee; I appreciate the opportunity to appear before you today.

On behalf of Secretary Kerry, I'd like to thank the Committee for holding today's hearing on wildlife trafficking. This is an issue of critical importance and one that the world cannot afford to stand idle on. This is a global challenge that spans continents and crosses oceans.

Wildlife trafficking is a multi-billion dollar criminal enterprise that has expanded from a conservation concern to an acute security threat. The increasing involvement of organized crime in poaching and wildlife trafficking promotes corruption, threatens the peace and security of fragile regions, strengthens illicit trade routes, destabilizes economies and communities that depend on wildlife for their livelihoods and contributes to the spread of disease.

The United States government has worked on this complex issue for decades, and is committed to ending this deadly practice. As you are all aware, President Obama released the *National Strategy for Combating Wildlife Trafficking* on February 11, 2014. The National Strategy is a key outcome of his July 1, 2013 Executive Order (E.O) 13648, which established an interagency Task Force to address this global problem, co-chaired by the Departments of State, Justice, and Interior. The National Strategy is the result of intensive discussions among principals of the Presidential Task Force on Wildlife Trafficking and identifies guiding principles and strategic priorities for U.S. efforts to stem illegal trade in wildlife. The *Strategy* further strengthens U.S. leadership on countering the global security threat posed by transnational criminal organizations that engage in illegal trade in wildlife. It sets three strategic priorities:

- o **Strengthening domestic and global enforcement**, including assessing the related laws, regulations, and enforcement tools;

- o **Reducing demand for illegally traded wildlife** at home and abroad; and,

- o **Building international cooperation and public-private partnerships to combat illegal wildlife poaching and trade.**

The Strategy addresses the corruption, cross-border trafficking and laundering of criminal proceeds related to wildlife trafficking. Our ongoing efforts to curb the illegal wildlife trade will be guided by five principles that we believe will be crucial to our success: marshalling the full breadth of federal resources; strategically deploying those resources; utilizing the best available information to make decisions; considering all links of the illegal trade chain; and strengthening our relationships with other governments and partners around the world to address this challenge.

One of the key elements of the Strategy is expanding U.S. ivory trade controls, thereby closing existing loopholes to achieve a near total ban on the commercial trade of elephant ivory in the United States. As a major consumer of wildlife products (both legal and illegal), this domestic action sends a powerful message to the world and is critical to the overall solution.

Although the U.S. government has an important role to play in addressing wildlife trafficking, it cannot solve this problem alone. The United States believes that we must work with our partners across sectors and around the globe if we are to find a global solution to this problem.

Secretary Kerry has long championed our efforts to combat wildlife trafficking and the State Department is pleased to be continuing to carry on and broaden our international efforts. State has for many years coordinated an interagency group focused on wildlife trafficking, and we have worked very closely across all parts of the Department and with our colleagues in USAID on this issue. The E.O. and Task Force have led to a higher-level of coordination and intensified focus that will allow us to more strategically and effectively combat this pernicious trade by building better synergies across agencies, reducing redundancies and identifying complimentary lines of effort. We continue to make significant headway to tackle wildlife trafficking since the release of Executive Order (E.O.) 13648 on July 1, 2013.

Strengthening Global Enforcement

Driven by high demand and high profits for wildlife and wildlife products, coupled with low risk of detection and often inadequate penalties, criminal syndicates and terrorist networks are increasingly drawn to wildlife trafficking, which generates revenues conservatively estimated at $8-10 billion per year. Rhino horn for example is currently worth more than gold or cocaine, yet in many parts of the world those caught engaging in wildlife trafficking may risk small fines or minimal jail sentencing. Illegal trade in fisheries resources threatens food security in coastal communities globally and has economic impacts of $10 to $23.5 billion every year. We're working to change that equation by encouraging other countries to impose stronger legislation, better enforcement, and stiffer penalties.

Recent enforcement success and ongoing efforts include:

- In January 2014, The United Nations Security Council adopted resolutions imposing sanctions on individuals and entities in connection with the crises in the Central African Republic and the Democratic Republic of the Congo; we worked closely with our mission in New York to ensure that wildlife trafficking was included as a basis for sanctions in both resolutions.

- With the strong support of Chairman Royce, in November 2013, Secretary Kerry announced the first reward under the Transnational Organized Crime Reward Program to combat wildlife trafficking. The reward offers up to $1 million for information leading to the dismantling of the Xaysavang Network, a transnational crime syndicate facilitating wildlife trafficking from Africa and Asia.

- The Department of State has long worked with foreign governments to enhance their capacity to fight wildlife trafficking, as well as within international fora and through our bilateral relationships to persuade our global partners to treat wildlife trafficking seriously. One such example is the U.S. delegation we led to the November 2013 China-U.S. Joint Liaison Group on Law Enforcement Cooperation (JLG) meeting, during which U.S. Co-Chairs proposed that the United States and China explore ways to cooperate further on wildlife trafficking.

- In July 2013, the United Nations Economic and Social Council adopted a resolution from the UN Commission on Crime Prevention and Criminal Justice (CCPCJ) – co-sponsored in the CCPCJ by the United States – encouraging member countries to make wildlife trafficking a serious crime as defined in the UN Convention against Transnational Organized Crime (TOC), which provides for enhanced international cooperation on extradition and other measures with respect to serious crimes.

- We are building law enforcement and criminal justice capacity and cooperation globally, to include East Asia and the Pacific and Latin America, aiming to strengthen policies and legislative frameworks and develop capacities to prosecute and adjudicate crimes related to wildlife trafficking.

- We continue to support the International Law Enforcement Academies in Gaborone, Botswana, and Bangkok, Thailand which have trained 350 law enforcement officers in wildlife crime investigations since 2002.

Together with the USAID, U.S. Fish and Wildlife Service (USFWS), and international partners, the State Department funded a global operation to combat wildlife poaching and trafficking, code-named "Operation Cobra 2," from December 2013 through January 2014. The month-long operation brought together police, customs, and wildlife officials from 28 countries, including China, the United States, as well as African and Southeast Asian nations, with international enforcement agencies. Together they staged the operation out of two coordination centers in Nairobi and Bangkok, with links to field operatives across Africa and Asia. The investigative operation promoted cross-border law enforcement cooperation and enhanced capacity, and resulted in more than 400 arrests of wildlife criminals and 350 major wildlife seizures across Africa and Asia.

For the last decade the State Department has partnered with other U.S. government agencies to stand up regional Wildlife Enforcement Networks (WENs) to tackle wildlife trafficking. The State Department and USAID are supporting the Association of Southeast Asian Nations ASEAN-WEN, the South Asia WEN, the Central America WEN, the Horn of Africa WEN, and other emerging WENs around the world, including efforts in Central Africa, South America, and

Southern Africa. In March 2013, we worked to strengthen enforcement and existing partnerships by hosting at the CITES COP the First Global Meeting of the Wildlife Enforcement Networks. Our goal is the creation of a global network of regional wildlife enforcement networks.

Since its launch in 2005, ASEAN-WEN has served as a model for other WENs and produced tangible results, such as an 11-fold increase in the number of wildlife trafficking related arrests and seizures by member states and trained more than 3,000 government officials in law enforcement techniques. In 2013 ASEAN member countries announced their commitment to ownership and leadership of the WEN, through financial contributions that will sustain the ASEAN-WEN when USAID funding to the Network's Program Coordination Unit phases out later in 2014.

USAID recently expanded its support to the National Strategy in FY14 for existing programs, such as the U.S. government's flagship counter wildlife trafficking program, Asia's Regional Response to Endangered Species Trafficking in Asia, and a new partnership with the Department of Interior for technical assistance to combat wildlife crime in Asia.

USAID is supporting Project PREDATOR, implemented by INTERPOL. Project PREDATOR focuses on stopping the illegal trade in Asian big cats such as tigers and snow leopards and aims to develop communication, cooperation and collaboration with respect to intelligence exchange, initiating cross-border investigations, and training among law enforcement officials.

Wildlife Trafficking in Sub-Saharan Africa

The United States recognizes the heavy toll that wildlife trafficking is taking in African nations, bringing some species to the brink of extinction. In 2013 alone an estimated 30,000 African elephants were killed for their ivory, more than 80 animals per day. Even starker is the decimation of forest elephant populations in Central Africa which have declined by approximately two-thirds between 2002 and 2012. Beyond this horrible slaughter, armed poachers kill hundreds of park rangers and eco-guards and threaten the very livelihoods of those who depend on these natural resources.

Thanks to the support of Congress, the Department of State is supporting law enforcement training and technical assistance to further efforts to combat wildlife trafficking in the region, including Kenya and South Africa, and other regional Sub-Saharan Africa programs. Foreign assistance will aim to strengthen policies and legislative frameworks; enhance investigative and law enforcement functions; support regional cooperation among enforcement agencies; and develop capacities to prosecute and adjudicate crimes related to wildlife trafficking. We are committed to do more and work smarter with partners around the world to support wildlife range states to maintain the integrity of their national borders and protect their iconic wildlife.

On February 12, President Obama reached agreement with his French counterpart, Francois Hollande, to work together to combat wildlife trafficking in Central Africa. As current facilitator for the Congo Basin Forest Partnership (CBFP), we devoted an extended session to the issue in the November 2013 CBFP Partners Meeting in November 2013; and we held an anti-poaching workshop in Gabon in 2012.

Another key effort in the region is the Central Africa Regional Program for the Environment (CARPE) which has greatly increased its focus on combating wildlife trafficking investing $9.8 million in FY13 funding on this issue. CARPE has increased investments combatting poaching and wildlife trafficking in each landscape, along transit routes and in major ports and cities, and at the policy level. For example, the SMART model for targeted patrolling is being introduced in each landscape, while a model for strengthening law enforcement, from arrest through prosecution, is being brought to Democratic Republic of Congo. These USAID-managed initiatives are complemented by USAID-funded grants and partnerships managed by the US Fish and Wildlife Service.

In East Africa, USAID has two ongoing programs that address wildlife trafficking and focus on the communities that live with wildlife and rely on healthy populations of elephant and other species for tourism. These programs are:

- In Kenya, USAID's over 15 years of work with conservancies and their game guards has been instrumental in addressing poaching in important wildlife areas outside of government conservation areas. USAID has been active in the wildlife policy for many years culminating in a new Policy in 2013. USAID continues to assist targeted efforts on implementation working with the Kenyan Wildlife Service and other relevant agencies.

- In Tanzania, USAID has been the lead funder over the last ten years of the Tanzanian conservancy model – Wildlife Management Areas (WMAs). This allows communities to benefit from wildlife on their land and aligns local incentives in favor of long-term conservation management. The WMAs are a key feature in addressing poaching in wildlife dispersal areas and game guard development.

Additionally, USAID is supporting anti-trafficking in Tanzania, focused on supporting national environmental policy and legislation, encouraging community-based natural resource management, and providing technical support to anti-poaching scouts. USAID/Tanzania works closely with USFWS on targeted efforts to address elephant poaching.

And in Southern Africa, the Department of State and USAID supported a workshop in Botswana in October 2013 that brought together key countries in the region to explore the creation of a Southern African Wildlife Enforcement Network (WEN-SA) to coordinate regional enforcement efforts, which is moving forward with broad regional buy-in.

Continent-wide, the State Department's International Visitor Leadership Program in 2013 held an exchange focused on anti-poaching and anti-trafficking best practices, connecting wildlife authorities and private sector stakeholders from key African countries with counterparts in the United States. U.S. Ambassadors in all sub-Saharan African countries and State Department principals continually push African leaders and senior government officials to take concrete steps to protect their wildlife, to prevent trafficking, and to put a stop to the corruption that enables the crimes to continue.

National Security Concerns

Poaching presents serious security challenges for militaries and police forces in a number of African nations, whose protective services are often outgunned by heavily-armed criminal operations. Once small-scale, poachers are increasingly sophisticated, targeting and killing animals with weapons including semiautomatic rifles and rocket-propelled grenades. Nature reserves, a major source of tourism income for many countries, are becoming increasingly militarized. Traffickers exploit porous borders and weak institutions to profit from trading in illegal wildlife. Wildlife and wildlife products are transported through multi-stage illicit networks of corrupt middlemen and officials. There is evidence that wildlife trafficking syndicates benefit from trafficking activities and may even drive them financially.

While underscoring transnational organized crime is important, we are also increasingly concerned with links to terrorists and rogue military personnel. Like many illicit activities, it is difficult to determine the extent to which these actors are involved. We believe, however, that the Lord's Resistance Army, the Janjaweed, and al-Shabaab have been at least partly involved. There is evidence that some insurgent groups are directly involved in poaching or trafficking, who then trade wildlife products for weapons or safe haven. We believe that, at a minimum, they are likely sharing some of the same facilitators – corrupt customs and border officials, money launderers, supply chains, etc.

We still have much to learn about the full extent of the relationship between suspected terrorist financing and wildlife trafficking. One of the goals of our assistance efforts is to promote greater information sharing and coordination within and among governments, law enforcement and intelligence agencies, conservation groups and other actors working in this area.

Recognizing these broader security implications, as part of the E.O. President Obama charged the Task Force to develop recommendations to apply the 2011 Strategy to Combat Transnational Organized Crime (TOC) to wildlife trafficking.

Reduce Demand for Illegally Traded Wildlife

Wildlife trafficking is a global problem that requires a global solution that addresses the supply, transit, and demand sides of the issue. Addressing demand is a complex and long-term issue, which depends in part on the species in question. It is not enough to increase public awareness. In order to end wildlife trafficking, the buying must stop.

Specific demand-reduction efforts include:

- USAID's "Asia Regional Response to Endangered Species Trafficking" (ARREST) project, which goes through 2016, has launched a series of strategically connected, Government-endorsed Demand Reduction Campaigns in Asia's three biggest wildlife market and transit countries, as well as first Asia-wide online/smartphone information-sharing platform that will help counter wildlife consumption.

- We funded a Public Service Announcement in partnership with the UN Office of Drugs and Crime, released in November 2013, featuring Chinese actress Li Bing Bing and addressing transnational organized crime and wildlife trafficking in Southeast Asia. Previously, State sponsored PSAs with conservationist Jane Goodall and actor Harrison Ford.

- We are encouraging our Embassies to host activities to commemorate the first ever March 3 World Wildlife Day. This effort will build upon public outreach activities undertaken by more than 54 U.S. Missions in our December 4, 2012, commemoration of "Wildlife Conservation Day."

International Cooperation, Commitment, and Public–Private Partnerships

When we discuss wildlife trafficking, we tend to think largely about Africa or Asia, but this is a truly global problem. No single country is the root of the wildlife trafficking problem and no one country can solve it alone. Governments around the world – including our own – are feeling the pressure, and we need to be proactive to stem this global problem. The combined efforts of all key stakeholders, including foreign government partners, non-governmental organizations, the private sector, and other elements of civil society, are needed to effectively address the problem. The United States is itself a major demand and transit country, and compels us to be part of the solution to addressing this global scourge.

To address the challenge of wildlife trafficking, the State Department collaborates closely with other U.S. government agencies, foreign governments, and the non-governmental community in various international fora, taking global, regional, and bilateral approaches to find innovative and sustainable solutions.

Combating wildlife trafficking requires the engagement of governments in range states as well as transit and consumer countries throughout the world. We will continue to promote commitments to conservation and to fighting the crime and corruption that fuels wildlife trafficking both within countries directly facing this challenge and across borders, among regions, and globally. The U.S. government will further use diplomacy to secure commitments in international fora and at the highest levels of governments. We will continue to strengthen and ensure the effective implementation of international agreements and arrangements and work toward new measures, as appropriate, to meet this evolving challenge.

We have advocated for countries to work together to combat wildlife trafficking in a number of multilateral fora, including the G-8, APEC, ASEAN, the UN Food and Agriculture Organization, and the UN Commission on Crime Prevention and Criminal Justice. We have also pressed multilateral institutions including the African Union, the African Development Bank, and Regional Economic Communities in Africa to take a more active stance against wildlife trafficking.

The Department was pleased to join the U.S. delegation, led by Associate Attorney General Tony West, to the London Conference on the Illegal Wildlife Trade hosted by U.K. Foreign Secretary William Hague February 12-13, 2014. We were pleased with the outcome of the Conference and the commitments contained in the Conference Declaration.

We led the U.S. delegation to the December 2013 International Union for Conservation of Nature (IUCN) African Elephant Summit in Botswana, where ministers and senior officials from key African elephant range states, as well as crucial transit and destination countries for trafficked ivory, committed to take urgent measures to halt the illegal trade and secure elephant populations across Africa. USAID supported the meeting through their Wildlife TRAPS program with IUCN.

I participated in two minister-level events on the margins of the September 2013 UN General Assembly, including one hosted by Gabon and Germany to explore options for greater involvement of UN entities in the fight against wildlife trafficking.

We continue to work with USTR to address the growing illegal trade in wildlife under the auspices of various U.S. Free Trade Agreements (FTAs), including in negotiations regarding the Transatlantic Trade and Investment Partnership (TTIP) and the Trans-Pacific Partnership (TPP).

We have actively engaged countries bilaterally as well. On February 17, Secretary Kerry and Indonesian Forest Minister Hasan signed a Memorandum of Understanding (MOU) on Conserving Wildlife and Combating Wildlife Trafficking in Jakarta. The MOU fosters bilateral cooperation in protecting critical habitat; building capacity to manage and conserve wildlife; incorporating scientific information into public awareness programs; strengthening conservation science and law enforcement; and stabilizing (and growing) populations of threatened and endangered species. This is the first MOU of its kind and a key step forward with Indonesia, one of the world's most biodiverse countries.

We have made strides in our bilateral engagement with China to combat wildlife trafficking over the last year. The United States and China destroyed approximately six tons each of our respective confiscated elephant ivory stockpiles. In addition to our global efforts to highlight the first ever World Wildlife Day on March 3 and raise awareness of the serious impacts of wildlife trafficking, we are coordinating separate events with the Chinese to celebrate the occasion.

Conclusion

Combating wildlife trafficking is a complex challenge which demands a multifaceted holistic and whole-of-government approach. To this end, this year the United States will support efforts to combat wildlife trafficking and to conserve biodiversity worldwide. Within the framework of the National Strategy, we will work across the U.S. government to focus our international investments to combat wildlife trafficking in the most strategic and effective way possible.

The Administration seeks an open and inclusive dialogue about the challenges presented by wildlife trafficking and possible ways to address those challenges. In coming months, we will work with the Advisory Council, set up under the Executive Order, and with other Task Force members to implement the National Strategy and collaborate where appropriate with NGOs, private sector partners, and other members of the public to ensure the strategy's success. At the same time, we will continue to work with international partners to address this global challenge.

In closing I would like to reiterate Secretary Kerry's continued commitment to tackling this illegal trade. He has long been a champion of our efforts to combat wildlife trafficking, including during his tenure as Chair of the Senate Foreign Relations Committee. We greatly appreciate the leadership that Congress has shown on this issue and for the support provided to enhance our ability to combat wildlife trafficking and dismantle the trans-national criminal organizations that profit from it. The support of Congress sends a powerful message to the world that we are united in our seriousness of purpose. We look forward to working with you in these efforts going forward.

I very much appreciate the opportunity to appear before you today and I would be happy to take any questions you may have.

Chairman ROYCE. Thank you, Doctor.
Mr. Ashe.

STATEMENT OF THE HONORABLE DANIEL M. ASHE, DIREC-TOR, U.S. FISH AND WILDLIFE SERVICE, U.S. DEPARTMENT OF THE INTERIOR

Mr. ASHE. Good morning, Chairman Royce, Ranking Member Bass, committee members. On behalf of Secretary Sally Jewell, I appreciate the opportunity to testify here today about the National Strategy for Combating Wildlife Trafficking.

Spurred by President Obama's Executive order, the strategy begins the process of leveraging resources and expertise across the Federal Government to crack down on the poaching and trafficking that is devastating some of the world's most beloved animals, evidence of that trafficking is on display here on the tabletop before us.

As recent events demonstrate, United States leadership is vital. Since we crushed the United States' stockpile of seized illegal ivory in November, China and France have followed suit, and Hong Kong has also announced its intention to do so.

At my right in front of Dr. Jones is a sample of the crushed ivory from our Denver event in November. In addition, this past year we concluded our most successful CITES conference ever with nine of the 10 U.S.-sponsored proposals gaining approval by member nations.

The Department of the Interior and the U.S. Fish and Wildlife Service will help lead the strategy's implementation with our colleagues in the Department of Justice and State, building on the foundation that has been laid through decades of international conservation and law enforcement work.

We have a four-tiered approach to combating wildlife trafficking with our international partners. First, we continue to work with international law enforcement agencies to disrupt and dismantle trafficking networks and arrest those responsible for the brutal slaughter of these magnificent creatures.

We have a photo, I think, showing some 1,500 raw tusks that were recently seized in Togo, the largest seizure yet by a West African nation, and perhaps that will be displayed in a moment.

We provide critical financial and technical support for on-the-ground conservation efforts and to build the capacity of range states to protect wildlife and bring poachers and traffickers to justice.

We work here in the United States and with our partners in Asia, Europe and Latin America to reduce demand for wildlife products and we continue working with CITES member nations to support sustainable trade and well-managed wildlife management programs that provide jobs and economic development opportunities in development range countries, as Ranking Member Bass was speaking to, thus reducing the allure of poaching and trafficking.

Now highlighting some of the strategy's most significant actions, we are using the full extent of our existing legal authority to stop virtually all commercial trade of elephant ivory and rhino horn within the United States and across its borders.

Just yesterday, I signed a Fish and Wildlife Service Director's Order 210, beginning the implementation of that effort. All commercial imports of African elephant ivory into the United States will be prohibited without exception.

Nearly all commercial exports of elephant ivory will also be prohibited with the exception of a very small, strictly defined, class of antiques with verified documentation of their antiquity.

Domestic commerce will be prohibited, again, with the exception of documented antiques and other items clearly documented as legally imported prior to the protection of the species under CITES Appendix 1.

The strategy also recommends the continued sale of the Save Vanishing Species semipostal stamp. The public has purchased more than 25.5 million stamps, generating more than $2.5 million for conservation of elephants, rhinoceros, tigers, marine turtles and great apes.

I want to conclude by asking you to consider this moment in history. Mr. Rohrabacher referenced the leadership that is being demonstrated here. We have a chance here and now to take action to ensure that elephants, rhinos and hundreds of other wild plant and animal species do not vanish from the wild.

Because of the President's leadership, that of good colleagues and friends and other great institutions and that of this great committee, we can dare to dream that our grandchildren will be able to see these iconic species, their heritage as global citizens, in their native habitat in the wild.

I look forward to working with your committee to help to make this dream a reality. Thank you, Mr. Chairman.

[The prepared statement of Mr. Ashe follows:]

TESTIMONY OF DAN ASHE, DIRECTOR, U.S. FISH AND WILDLIFE SERVICE, DEPARTMENT OF THE INTERIOR, BEFORE THE U.S. HOUSE OF REPRESENTATIVES, COMMITTEE ON FOREIGN AFFAIRS, REGARDING THE NATIONAL STRATEGY FOR COMBATING WILDLIFE TRAFFICKING

February 26, 2014

Introduction

Good morning Chairman Royce, Ranking Member Engel, and Members of the Committee. I am Dan Ashe, Director of the U.S. Fish and Wildlife Service (Service), within the Department of the Interior (Department). I appreciate the opportunity to testify before you today to discuss the National Strategy for Combating Wildlife Trafficking.

The Service provides key leadership and capacity in addressing wildlife trafficking. For decades, we have worked in countries across the globe to conserve imperiled wildlife and address illicit wildlife trade. The Service's responsibilities include certain international conservation efforts, administered by our International Affairs program. The Service's Office of Law Enforcement, which is essential to wildlife conservation, also plays a key role in international conservation, including combating illegal wildlife trafficking.

The Wildlife Trafficking Crisis

Illegal wildlife trade is estimated to be a multibillion-dollar business involving the unlawful harvest of and trade in live animals and plants or parts and products derived from them. Wildlife is traded as skins, leather goods or souvenirs; as food or traditional medicine; as pets; and in many other forms. Illegal wildlife trade runs the gamut from illegal logging of protected forests to supply the demand for exotic woods, to the illegal fishing of marine life for food, and the poaching of elephants to meet the demand for ivory. Illegal wildlife trade is typically unsustainable, harming wild populations of animals and plants, and pushing endangered species toward extinction. Endangered animals and plants are often the target of wildlife crime because of their rarity and high economic value. Furthermore, wildlife trafficking negatively impacts a country's natural resources and local communities that might otherwise benefit from tourism or legal, sustainable trade.

Wildlife trafficking once was predominantly a crime of opportunity committed by individuals or small groups. Today, it is the purview of international criminal cartels that are well structured and highly organized, and capable of illegally moving orders of magnitude more in wildlife and wildlife products. This lucrative business has been tied to drug and human trafficking organizations and is a destabilizing influence in many African nations. What was once a local or regional problem has become a global crisis, as increasingly sophisticated, violent, and ruthless criminal organizations have branched into wildlife trafficking. Organized criminal enterprises are a growing threat to wildlife, the world's economy, and global security.

Thousands of wildlife species are threatened by illegal and unsustainable wildlife trade. For example, in recent months significant media attention has gone to the plight of the world's rhinoceros species, which are facing increased poaching as demand for their horns increases in Asia. In some parts of Asia, rhino horn is considered to be a powerful traditional medicine, used to treat a variety of ailments. More recently, demand has shifted to less traditional uses, including as a cure for cancer or even as a hangover remedy, particularly in Vietnam. While there is little or no scientific evidence to support these claims, the dramatic rise in poaching to satisfy this demand is pushing rhinos toward the brink of extinction.

We have also seen a recent resurgence of elephant poaching in Africa, which is threatening this iconic species. Africa's elephants are being slaughtered for ivory at rates not seen in decades. Populations of both savannah and forest elephants have dropped precipitously, and poaching occurs across all regions of Africa. There is also a terrible human cost associated with these losses. During the past few years, hundreds of park rangers have been killed in the line of duty in Africa.

Improved economic conditions in markets such as China and other parts of East and Southeast Asia are fueling an increased demand for rhino horn, elephant ivory, and other wildlife products. More Asian consumers have the financial resources to purchase these wildlife products, which are a status symbol for new economic elites. Although the primary markets are in Asia, the United States continues to play a role as a consumer and transit country for illegally traded wildlife, and we must be a part of the solution.

President's Executive Order on Wildlife Trafficking

The Administration recognized that if illicit wildlife trade continues on its current trajectory some of the world's most treasured animals could be threatened with extinction. We have a moral obligation to respond, and there is a key role for the U.S. Government to play. The criminals have raised their game, and we must do the same. In response to this crisis, on July 1, 2013, President Obama issued Executive Order 13648 to enhance coordination of U.S. Government efforts to combat wildlife trafficking and assist foreign governments with capacity building. Upon issuing the Executive Order, President Obama said, "We need to act now to reverse the effects of wildlife trafficking on animal populations before we lose the opportunity to prevent the extinction of iconic animals like elephants and rhinoceroses."

The Executive Order establishes a Presidential Task Force on Wildlife Trafficking charged with developing and implementing a National Strategy for Combating Wildlife Trafficking. The Task Force is co-chaired by the Department of the Interior, Department of Justice, and Department of State, and includes a dozen other departments and agencies. Drawing on resources and expertise from across the U.S. Government, we are working to identify new approaches to crack down on poaching and wildlife trafficking and to more efficiently coordinate our enforcement efforts with interagency and international partners.

The Executive Order also establishes an Advisory Council on Wildlife Trafficking comprised of individuals with relevant expertise from outside the Government to make recommendations to the Task Force. The Service, along with the co-chairing agencies, are engaging the Council's expertise in law enforcement and criminal justice, wildlife biology and conservation, finance and trade, and international relations and diplomacy to develop and advance this national strategy.

U.S. Fish and Wildlife Service's Role in Addressing Wildlife Trafficking

I would like to highlight the National Strategy for Combating Wildlife Trafficking and how we in the Service are strengthening our efforts to address this critical issue. But first, I would like to discuss the Service's ongoing efforts over the past few decades working across the globe to conserve imperiled wildlife and address illicit wildlife trade. We have a four-tiered approach to combat wildlife trafficking with our international partners. The approach focuses on: law enforcement; technical assistance; the Convention on International Trade in Endangered Species of Wild Fauna and Flora (CITES); and demand reduction.

<u>Law Enforcement to Target and Stop Illicit Trade</u>

The Service is the primary Federal agency responsible for enforcing U.S. laws and treaties that address international wildlife trafficking and protect U.S. and foreign species from unsustainable trade. Working with shoestring budgets and a special agent workforce that has not grown since the late-1970s, the Service has disrupted large-scale trafficking in contraband wildlife "commodities" that range from elephant ivory and rhino horn to sturgeon caviar and sea turtle skin and shell.

Service special agents utilize both overt and clandestine investigative techniques to detect and document international smuggling and crimes involving the unlawful exploitation of protected native and foreign species in interstate commerce. A wildlife smuggling investigation typically involves securing charges under both the Endangered Species Act (ESA) (a misdemeanor statute) and the felony wildlife trafficking provisions of the Lacey Act (where the Federal felony violation is predicated on the violation of another Federal, State, foreign, or tribal wildlife law). Such investigations also often document and secure felony charges for related crimes such as conspiracy, smuggling, money laundering, false statements, and wire fraud.

Since the mid-1970s, the Service has deployed a force of uniformed wildlife inspectors at major ports of entry across the nation to check inbound and outbound shipments for wildlife. These 130 officers ensure that wildlife trade complies with the CITES treaty and U.S. laws. They also conduct proactive inspections of air cargo warehouses, ocean containers, international mail packages, and international passenger flights looking for smuggled wildlife. Discoveries by wildlife inspectors at the ports may lead to full-scale criminal investigations of wildlife trafficking.

The Service operates the world's first and only full-service wildlife forensics laboratory – a lab that is globally recognized as having created the science of wildlife forensics. Guidance from the lab, for example, provided an easy way for officers in the field to distinguish elephant ivory from other types of ivory, such as mammoth or walrus ivory. The Service continues to support a FY14 budget request to expand research at our lab to make it easier to determine the origin or geographic source of illicit wildlife material, particularly for species threatened by current patterns of illegal trade. Such evidence enhances our ability to provide law enforcement and justice officials with evidence to more effectively prosecute wildlife crime.

Service enforcement officers and forensic scientists have provided specialized training to wildlife enforcement counterparts in more than 65 different countries since 2000. These capacity-building efforts have included teaching criminal investigation skills to wildlife officers from sub-Saharan Africa at the International Law Enforcement Academy in Botswana on a yearly or twice-yearly basis.

One example of the Service's law enforcement efforts in combating wildlife trafficking is Operation Crash. This Operation is an ongoing nationwide criminal investigation led by the Service that is addressing all aspects of U.S. involvement in the black market rhino horn trade. The first phase of this probe, which has focused on the unlawful purchase and outbound smuggling of rhino horn from the United States, has resulted in 15 arrests and nine convictions to date. Charges filed against these defendants include conspiracy, smuggling, money laundering, tax evasion, bribery, and making false documents as well as violations of the ESA and Lacey Act. Eight of those arrested were taken into custody in February 2012 as part of a nationwide "takedown" that involved more than 140 law enforcement officers executing search warrants in 13 States. Successes in 2013 include the arrests and indictments of several other individuals (including Chinese and U.S. antiques dealers) who were operating a second large-scale rhino horn and elephant ivory smuggling network.

Wildlife trafficking is increasingly a transnational crime involving illicit activities in two or more countries and often two or more global regions. Cooperation between nations is essential to combating this crime. Investigations of transnational crime are inherently difficult, and among other endeavors, the U.S. Government places U.S. law enforcement officials overseas to help combat such transnational crime. In January 2014, with assistance from the State Department and USAID, the Service created the first program for stationing special agents at U.S. embassies as international attachés, to coordinate investigations of wildlife trafficking and support wildlife enforcement capacity building. In collaboration with our State Department colleagues, the Service secured the first positions ever for FWS experts to be posted in embassies in Bangkok and Dar es Salaam, where they will coordinate investigations of wildlife trafficking and support wildlife enforcement capacity building. Additional postings in key regions are planned in the coming year.

Technical Assistance and Grants to Build In-Country Capacity

The Service has a long history of providing technical assistance and grants to build in-country capacity for conservation of wildlife species. Through the Multinational Species Conservation Funds, the Service provides funding in the form of grants or cooperative agreements to projects benefiting African and Asian elephants, rhinos, tigers, great apes, and marine turtles in their natural habitats. A substantial portion of the funding awarded through the Multinational Species Conservation Funds is invested in projects aimed at combating wildlife crime through improved law enforcement, anti-poaching patrols, demand reduction, and economic alternatives. Several of the Service's global and regional programs, including Africa, Asia, and the Western Hemisphere, also directly address wildlife conservation efforts, including combating wildlife crime.

Through the Wildlife Without Borders – Africa Program, a technical and financial partnership with USAID, the Service has supported the development of innovative methods to conserve wildlife and fight wildlife crime in Central Africa, including improvement of investigations, arrest operations, and legal follow-up. A number of projects are geared toward building in-country capacity and providing technical assistance to reduce the poaching of African elephants, which once numbered in the millions but are now estimated at fewer than 400,000 across the continent. The Service is committed to working with in-country partners to halt and reverse this trend, most notably in Gabon, where two-thirds of the forest elephants in Minkebe National Park have been killed since 2004, a loss of more than 11,000 elephants. This includes a 5-year cooperative agreement with the Gabonese National Parks Agency totaling more than $3.1 million and matched by more than $3.3 million in additional leveraged funds.

In Latin America, the Service is working with partners to reduce the trafficking of species such as macaws and other parrots, jaguars, and reptiles through law enforcement training efforts in Mexico. Grant funding also supports the expansion of income-generating programs to communities in Colombia as an alternative to the illegal pet trade. Throughout Africa and Asia, funding is supporting conservation efforts to reduce the demand for ivory, rhino horn, tigers, pangolins, and other endangered wildlife by targeting government decision-makers, young people, and the business sector through awareness campaigns.

Through the Critically Endangered Animal Fund and the Amphibians in Decline Fund, projects around the world are protecting endangered animals and amphibians from poaching and illegal wildlife trade. From Snow Leopards in Pakistan to Peru's Lake Titicaca frogs, these two funds are supporting projects that are helping to save these animals.

This is a pivotal moment in the conservation movement. We are now witnessing a confluence of two forces – an alarming, unprecedented, and dramatic increase in the slaughter of wildlife coupled with dramatic increases in trafficking and poaching. Species decline is being exacerbated by the lack of law enforcement coupled with corruption, instability, and underlying poverty. These grants provide critical conservation support across the globe for numerous endangered species.

CITES and Illegal Wildlife Trade

CITES, an international agreement among 180 member nations, including the United States, is designed to control and regulate global trade in certain wild animals and plants that are or may become threatened with extinction due to international trade. . As the first nation to ratify CITES, the United States has consistently been a leader in combating wildlife trafficking and protecting natural resources. More than 35,000 species currently benefit from CITES protection. International trade in plants and animals, whether taken from the wild or bred in captivity, can pose serious risks to species. Without regulation, international trade can deplete wild populations, leading to extinction. The goal of CITES is to facilitate legal, biologically sustainable trade, whenever possible. But in some cases, no level of commercial trade can be supported.

Though a longstanding priority for CITES Parties, the focus on combating elephant poaching and illegal ivory trade is more intense than ever before. In March 2013, at the most recent meeting of the Conference of the Parties (CoP16), eight countries—China, Kenya, Malaysia, the Philippines, Tanzania, Thailand, Uganda, and Viet Nam—that were identified as significant source, transit, or destination points for illegal ivory trade agreed to develop time-bound action plans to actively address illegal ivory trade.

Also at CoP16, the CITES Parties recognized the importance of addressing the entire crime chain by adopting several decisions to ensure that modern forensic and investigative techniques are applied to the illegal trade in ivory. The CITES Parties agreed to provide more effective control over domestic ivory markets and government-held stockpiles, and to promote public awareness campaigns, including supply and demand-reduction strategies.

The decisions agreed upon at CoP16 to address the elephant poaching crisis were a significant step in the right direction. The United States played a major role in the development of all of these decisions and actions, and is committed to playing a significant role in their implementation, including ensuring that countries are held accountable for failure to do so.

Reducing Consumer Demand for Illegal Wildlife Products

Most of the international conservation work funded by the Service has focused on on-the-ground protection of habitat and wildlife, including enforcement efforts, with the Service providing approximately $10 million annually to enhance and support wildlife conservation throughout Africa and Asia. In addition, the Service supports government and non-government partners in consumer nations in Asia in public awareness and demand-reduction campaigns.

Over the years, the Service has also worked to educate and inform U.S. consumers about the role they play in wildlife trafficking and the impacts of this illegal activity on animal and plant species around the world. These efforts have ranged from partnering with nongovernmental organizations on a long-running "Buyer Beware" campaign and commissioning our law enforcement officers to present outreach programs on wildlife trafficking at the local, State, and national levels, to using airport billboards and social media to engage the public on this issue.

The Service will play a key role in efforts going forward to reduce demand for illegally traded wildlife. Using our extensive network and diverse experience, we are developing a strategy for the Service's role in addressing consumer demand. This includes working with the private sector and governments in key consumer countries; building public awareness about the impacts of illegal trade on wild populations and the potential penalties for engaging in such activities; and taking other actions to encourage attitudinal and behavioral shifts, all leading to measurable reductions in demand for illegal wildlife products.

U.S. Ivory Crush

As part of our effort to combat illegal ivory trafficking, on November 14, 2013, the United States destroyed its 6-ton stock of confiscated elephant ivory, sending a clear message that we will not tolerate wildlife crime that threatens to wipe out the African elephant and a host of other species around the globe. The destruction of this ivory, which took place near the Service's National

Wildlife Property Repository on the Rocky Mountain Arsenal National Wildlife Refuge near Denver, Colorado, was witnessed by representatives of African nations and other countries, dozens of leading conservationists, and international media representatives.

This ivory crush sparked a new sense of possibility and collaboration—that we can work together effectively to halt this crisis before it is too late. We are now are in a much better position to work with the international community to push for a reduction of ivory stockpiles worldwide, and to crack down on poaching and illegal trade. The ivory crush signaled the United States' commitment to combating wildlife trafficking and one of the goals was to encourage other nations to do the same.

On January 6, 2014, the People's Republic of China destroyed more than 6 tons of illegal elephant ivory in the city of Guangzhou, Guangdong Province. On February 6, 2014, France's Ministry of Ecology, Sustainable Development and Energy announced the destruction of approximately 3 tons of ivory seized by customs and other law enforcement officials. Hong Kong has announced plans to do the same. These countries join the United States, Kenya, Gabon, and the Philippines, all of which have destroyed their illegal ivory, in this fight to save African elephants from poachers and the illegal ivory trade.

National Strategy for Combating Wildlife Trafficking

In accordance with the Executive Order, the Presidential Task Force produced a National Strategy for Combating Wildlife Trafficking. The National Strategy establishes strategic priorities and guiding principles to help focus and strengthen the U.S. Government's efforts to combat wildlife trafficking, and to position the United States to exercise leadership on this urgent issue.

The strategic priorities include: (1) strengthening the enforcement of laws and the implementation of international agreements that protect wildlife; (2) reducing demand for illegal wildlife and wildlife products; and (3) working in partnership with governments, local communities, non-governmental organizations, the private sector, and others to enhance global commitment to combat wildlife trafficking.

The Service is integrally involved in all of these priorities, but we would like to highlight a few areas of particular importance in our efforts to stem illegal wildlife trade.

Administrative Actions to Address the Current Poaching Crisis

The United States has several laws and regulations in place that can help to address the poaching crisis. African elephants are listed as threatened under the ESA and also protected under the African Elephant Conservation Act. Nations across the world regulate trade in this species under CITES. Under these U.S. laws, it is generally illegal to:

- Import or export African elephant ivory for primarily commercial purposes.
- Import or export it for other purposes without CITES documents.
- Buy or sell unlawfully imported African elephant ivory in interstate commerce.

Asian elephants are listed as endangered under the ESA. Import, export, and interstate commerce in ivory and other parts and products is generally prohibited.

Though there are several laws and regulations in place to address illegal trade, a number of loopholes exist that are exploited by illegal ivory traders. To more effectively combat illegal ivory trade, the Service is proposing to immediately pursue a series of administrative actions to establish a nearly complete U.S. ban on elephant ivory and rhino horn trade.

We will strengthen controls on the commercial import of African elephant ivory by eliminating broad administrative exceptions to the 1989 African Elephant Conservation Act moratorium. We will ensure that African elephants receive the same protections as other threatened and endangered species by revoking the regulatory exemption that allows African elephant ivory to be traded in ways that would otherwise be prohibited by the ESA. We will also limit the number of elephant sport-hunted trophies that an individual can import to two per person per year. In addition, we will improve protections that the ESA provides for all species listed as threatened or endangered by clarifying the regulations that implement the statute's exemptions for commercial trade of 100-year-old antiques. Finally, we will improve our ability to protect elephants, rhinos, and other CITES-listed wildlife by finalizing a proposed rule clarifying the existing "use after import" provisions in U.S. CITES regulations. Under this new rule, items such as elephant ivory and rhino horn imported for noncommercial purposes may not subsequently be sold in either intrastate or interstate commerce.

The combined result of these administrative actions would be the virtual elimination of all commercial trade (import, export, and interstate and intrastate sale) in elephant ivory and rhino horn, with certain narrow exceptions (e.g., ivory or rhino horn imported for law enforcement purposes). Taking these measures will establish U.S. leadership and support diplomatic efforts to encourage demand reduction in consumer nations.

The United States is one of the world's major consumers of illicit wildlife products, and we must lead by example. We also believe these actions are consistent with recent CITES recommendations adopted at the most recent meeting of the Conference of the Parties (CoP16).

Assess and Strengthen Legal Authorities

While the Service is pursuing administrative actions to address the poaching crisis, the National Strategy also identifies the need to analyze and assess in general the laws, regulations, and enforcement tools that are now, or could be, used to combat wildlife trafficking. The goal is to determine which are most effective and identify those that require strengthening.

In particular, the National Strategy calls on Congress to consider legislation to recognize wildlife trafficking crimes as predicate offenses for money laundering. This action would be invaluable to the Service's law enforcement efforts because it would place wildlife trafficking on an equal footing with other serious crimes. It would also provide our special agents with the same tools to investigate serious crimes that other federal law enforcement agencies have. This legislative change would help take the profit out of the illegal wildlife trade and end the days of wildlife trafficking being a low-risk, high-profit crime. Strong penalties provide a deterrent and assist the U.S. Government in unraveling complex conspiracies and combating trafficking. Offenders facing significant penalties are more likely to become key cooperating defendants than those facing a light penalty.

Save the Vanishing Species Semipostal Stamp

The National Strategy recommends continuing the sale of the Save the Vanishing Species Semipostal stamp. This stamp, which went on sale on September 20, 2011, has been providing vital support for the Service's efforts to fight global wildlife trafficking and poaching. More than 25.5 million stamps have been purchased in the United States by the public online and at their local post offices, generating more than $2.5 million for conservation. This money has been used to support 47 projects in 31 countries in Africa, Asia, and Latin America to conserve elephants, rhinoceroses, tigers, marine turtles, and great apes. These funds have been leveraged by an additional $3.6 million in matching contributions—making the stamp a key part of the United States' response to protecting wildlife and addressing the ongoing worldwide epidemic of poaching and wildlife trafficking.

The continued sale of the Save the Vanishing Species Semipostal stamp would extend an opportunity for the American public to support wildlife conservation abroad by directly contributing money to help rhinos, tigers, elephants, sea turtles, and great apes.

Conclusion

I would like to thank the Committee for your support of our efforts to combat wildlife trafficking. We look forward to continuing to work with you as we move from the National Strategy into the implementation phase. The National Strategy is a starting point rather than an end point. We will be developing an implementation plan and identifying which agencies are responsible for carrying out specific actions, and we will engage your Committee, as well as other Committees as appropriate, as we move forward.

I want to leave you by asking you to consider this moment in history—and the choice we must all make as human beings and global citizens. We have a chance here, and now, to build on this National Strategy to ensure a secure future for elephants, rhinos, and hundreds of other wild plant and animal species. How will we answer when our grandchildren ask why some of these magnificent creatures no longer exist in the wild? I want to be able to tell them that the Service did everything we could to keep these amazing species from vanishing from our planet. I look forward to working with your Committee to make it a reality.

Thank you for the opportunity to present testimony today. I would be pleased to answer any questions that you may have.

Chairman ROYCE. Thank you.

Mr. Dreher.

STATEMENT OF MR. ROBERT G. DREHER, ACTING ASSISTANT ATTORNEY GENERAL, ENVIRONMENT AND NATURAL RESOURCES DIVISION, U.S. DEPARTMENT OF JUSTICE

Mr. DREHER. Chairman Royce, Ranking Member Bass and members of the Committee on Foreign Affairs——

Chairman ROYCE. Let us try it one more time on punching that button.

Mr. DREHER. Okay.

Chairman ROYCE. There we go.

Mr. DREHER. That seems to be working.

Chairman Royce, Ranking Member Bass and members of the Committee on Foreign Affairs, thank you for the opportunity to appear before you today to discuss the work with the Department of Justice regarding wildlife trafficking.

The Department of Justice has long been a leader in the fight against wildlife trafficking and we are deeply engaged in the administration's efforts to combat wildlife trafficking and implement the National Strategy.

Earlier this month, Associate Attorney General Tony West led the U.S. delegation at the London conference on illegal wildlife trade at which more than 40 countries agreed to a declaration on the need for international action to address this crisis.

And the Department of Justice served as a co-chair along with my fellow co-chairs from the Department of State and Department of Interior and worked closely with 14 other Federal agencies to develop the National Strategy.

As the strategy recognizes, strong enforcement is critical to stopping those who kill and traffic in protected species. The environmental crime section of the Department of Justice works with the U.S. Attorneys Offices around the country and with our Federal agency partners to enforce the Lacey Act and the Endangered Species Act as well as statutes prohibiting smuggling, criminal conspiracy and related crimes.

In our prosecutions we are increasingly seeing the involvement of criminal organizations, including transnational criminal organizations, that may threaten the security interests of the United States and its allies.

We are currently involved, for example, in prosecuting cases developed through Operation Crash, an ongoing multi agency effort with very strong involvement of the investigative agents of the Fish and Wildlife Service and other Federal agencies including Customs and Border Patrol, to detect and prosecute those engaged in illegal killing of rhinoceros and the trafficking of rhinoceros horn. This initiative has resulted in multiple convictions, significant jail time, penalties and forfeited assets.

Recent Operation Crash cases involve organized criminal elements that speak to the scope and scale of this problem. In one such case, Zhifei Li, a Chinese national, pled guilty this past December to organizing a conspiracy in which at least 30 raw rhinoceros horns and numerous objects made from rhino horn and elephant ivory worth more than $4.5 million were smuggled illegally from the United States to China.

Li admitted that he was the boss of several antique dealers in the United States who helped him obtain and smuggle wildlife items and that he supplied ivory to three illegal-carving factories in China.

In another case, Michael Slattery, Jr., an Irish national, was recently sentenced to serve 14 months incarceration as well as to pay a fine and forfeit proceeds from his illegal trade in rhinoceros horn.

He admitted to illegal trafficking throughout the United States and is alleged to belong to an organized criminal group engaged in rhino horn trafficking.

We have seen success in prosecuting those illegal—who illegally traffic in elephant ivory including, for example, a defendant whose import-export businesses were fronts for smuggling into the United States products from endangered and protected wildlife species including raw elephant ivory.

Another ivory case concerned a 2-year criminal conspiracy in which six defendants pleaded guilty to illegally importing ivory through the New York's JFK Airport.

In our cases, we seek substantial penalties including incarceration appropriate for crimes of this magnitude. Strong enforcement in the United States is not enough, however. As the National Strategy recognizes, wildlife trafficking is a global problem that requires a global solution.

For that reason, the Department of Justice has for many years worked closely with other Federal agencies to help foreign governments build their capacity to develop and effectively enforce their own wildlife trafficking laws.

Our efforts in this area include training our foreign counterparts on the legal, investigative, prosecutorial and judicial aspects of enforcing wildlife laws.

We seek to help our partners craft strong laws, strengthen their investigation and evidence-gathering capabilities and improve their judicial and prosecutorial effectiveness.

I temporarily lost my place but I am soon about to recover it.

Chairman ROYCE. Feel free to summarize.

Mr. DREHER. Well, let me just say that we are very proud of our record of achievement in this area. The National Strategy is a reminder that much more is needed. The strategy calls for Federal coordination through a whole of government approach and is a strong basis for our continued movement forward.

We will commit our efforts to the prosecution of wildlife criminals and give it—treat it with the seriousness that these crimes warrant and deserve. We look forward to working with Congress to strengthen existing laws and to adopt new legislation to improve the tools available to address this challenge.

We welcome the longstanding interest of the members of this committee and others in the House and Senate in addressing this crisis, and thank you for the opportunity to participate.

Thank you.

[The prepared statement of Mr. Dreher follows:]

Department of Justice

STATEMENT

OF

ROBERT G. DREHER
ACTING ASSISTANT ATTORNEY GENERAL
ENVIRONMENT AND NATURAL RESOURCES DIVISION

BEFORE THE

COMMITTEE ON FOREIGN AFFAIRS
U.S. HOUSE OF REPRESENTATIVES

HEARING ENTITLED

"INTERNATIONAL WILDLIFE TRAFFICKING THREATS TO
CONSERVATION AND NATIONAL SECURITY"

PRESENTED ON

FEBRUARY 26, 2014

STATEMENT OF
ROBERT G. DREHER
ACTING ASSISTANT ATTORNEY GENERAL
ENVIRONMENT AND NATURAL RESOURCES DIVISION
DEPARTMENT OF JUSTICE

BEFORE THE
COMMITTEE ON FOREIGN AFFAIRS
U.S. HOUSE OF REPRESENTATIVES

"INTERNATIONAL WILDLIFE TRAFFICKING THREATS TO
CONSERVATION AND NATIONAL SECURITY"

Presented on
February 26, 2014

I.   INTRODUCTION

Chairman Royce, Representative Engel, and Members of the Committee on Foreign
Affairs, thank you for the opportunity to appear before you today to discuss the work of the
Environment and Natural Resources Division of the U.S. Department of Justice ("ENRD" or the
"Division") with respect to the Administration's efforts to combat wildlife trafficking. I have the
privilege to serve as the Acting Assistant Attorney General for ENRD, and I am grateful for the
opportunity to represent the interests of the United States.

II.   OVERVIEW OF THE ENVIRONMENT AND NATURAL RESOURCES
DIVISION

The Environment and Natural Resources Division is a core litigating component of the
U.S. Department of Justice (the "Department"). Founded more than a century ago, it has built a
distinguished record of legal excellence. The Division is organized into nine litigating sections
(Appellate; Environmental Crimes; Environmental Defense; Environmental Enforcement; Indian
Resources; Land Acquisition; Law and Policy; Natural Resources; and Wildlife and Marine
Resources), and an Executive Office that provides administrative support. ENRD has a staff of
over 600, more than 400 of whom are attorneys.

The Division functions as the Nation's environmental lawyer, representing virtually
every federal agency in courts across the United States and its territories and possessions in civil
and criminal cases that arise under an array of federal statutes. Our work furthers the
Department's strategic goals to prevent crime and enforce federal laws, defend the interests of
the United States, promote national security, and ensure the fair administration of justice at the
federal, state, local and tribal levels.

III.   ENRD'S WORK WITH RESPECT TO WILDLIFE TRAFFICKING

For the purposes of today's hearing, I would like to highlight the work of the Division in the areas of prosecuting wildlife and wildlife-related crimes; conducting capacity building and training in this area; and the Division's role in developing and, going forward, implementing the National Strategy for Combating Wildlife Trafficking.

The Department of Justice, principally through the work of the Environment Division, has long been a leader in the fight against wildlife trafficking.   Combating wildlife trafficking is a top priority for the Department. Earlier this month Associate Attorney General Tony West led the United States delegation at the London Conference on the Illegal Wildlife Trade, where high-level representatives from more than 40 countries gathered and issued a declaration emphasizing that urgent action is necessary to end wildlife trafficking and eliminate demand through high-level political commitment and international cooperation.

The Division has a separate section devoted to the prosecution of environmental crimes, including wildlife crime. The Environmental Crimes Section has 35 dedicated criminal prosecutors who often work together with U.S. Attorneys' Offices around the country and our federal agency partners (such as the U.S. Fish and Wildlife Service and the National Oceanic and Atmospheric Administration) in the area of wildlife trafficking. Our cases enforce the Endangered Species Act and the Lacey Act, as well as statutes prohibiting smuggling, criminal conspiracy, and related crimes. We have had significant successes over the years prosecuting smugglers and traffickers in: elephant ivory, endangered rhino horns, South African leopard, Asian and African tortoises and reptiles, and many other forms of protected wildlife. Some cases that exemplify these critical enforcement efforts are discussed below.

The Department also works in the international sphere by assisting and working with enforcement partners in source, transit, and destination countries for illegal trade in protected wildlife. The Department works in close collaboration with the State Department and various international organizations to promote more proactive international law enforcement operations, including through efforts to train investigators, prosecutors, and judges. Some examples of these activities are discussed in more detail below.

Most recently, the Department of Justice has engaged deeply in the Administration's effort to combat wildlife trafficking in its role as one of the three agency co-chairs of the Presidential Task Force on Wildlife Trafficking, established by President Obama's July 1, 2013 Executive Order on Combating Wildlife Trafficking. I had the honor of serving as a Task Force co-chair (as the Attorney General's delegate) and working with the other co-chairs from the Departments of State and the Interior, and the other Task Force agencies, to craft the National Strategy for Combating Wildlife Trafficking. The Strategy was announced by the White House on February 11, 2014 and it identifies three key priority areas: (1) strengthening domestic and global enforcement; (2) reducing demand for illegally traded wildlife at home and abroad; and (3) strengthening partnerships with foreign governments, international organizations, NGOs, local communities, private industry, and others to combat illegal wildlife poaching and trade. I discuss below the Department's role with respect to these key objectives.

A.   Wildlife Trafficking Prosecutions

The two primary federal anti-wildlife trafficking statutes that the Department enforces are the Lacey Act and the Endangered Species Act. The Lacey Act reaches two broad categories of wildlife offenses: illegal trafficking in wildlife and false labeling. The Endangered Species Act establishes a U.S. program for the conservation of endangered and threatened species. The Endangered Species Act makes it illegal to traffic in listed endangered or threatened species without a permit and also implements our international treaty obligations under the Convention on International Trade in Endangered Species of Wild Fauna and Flora (CITES)—a treaty establishing limits on trade in certain species of wildlife.

The types of cases we prosecute for illegal trafficking are varied. While many involve individuals trafficking in illegal wildlife and wildlife parts, we are also seeing the involvement of criminal organizations, including transnational criminal organizations that may threaten the security interests of the U.S. and its allies. We routinely seek punishment that includes sentences for significant periods of incarceration, fines, and restitution or community service to help mitigate harm caused by the offense; forfeiture of the wildlife and instrumentalities used to commit the offense; and, where wildlife traffickers also violate laws against smuggling or other related crimes, disgorgement of the proceeds of the illegal conduct.

A prominent example of the Division's robust prosecution of illegal wildlife trafficking is "Operation Crash," an ongoing multi-agency effort to detect, deter, and prosecute those engaged in the illegal killing of rhinoceros and the illegal trafficking of endangered rhinoceros horns. This initiative has resulted in multiple convictions, significant jail time, penalties, and asset forfeiture. In one case, *United States v. Zhifei Li* (D.N.J), the defendant pled guilty on December 20, 2013, to organizing an illegal wildlife smuggling conspiracy in which 30 raw rhinoceros horns and numerous objects made from rhino horn and elephant ivory (worth more than $4.5 million) were smuggled from the United States to China. Li pleaded guilty to a total of 11 counts: one count of conspiracy to smuggle and conspiracy to violate the Lacey Act, six smuggling violations, one Lacey Act trafficking violation, and two counts of making false wildlife documents. Li admitted that he was the "boss" of three antique dealers in the United States whom he paid to help obtain wildlife items and smuggle to him through Hong Kong. One of those individuals was Qiang Wang, aka "Jeffrey Wang," who was sentenced to serve 37 months' incarceration for smuggling Asian artifacts, including "libation cups," made from rhinoceros horn and ivory (*United States v. Qiang Wang* (S.D.N.Y.)). More information about the Li case is available at http://www.justice.gov/opa/pr/2013/December/13-enrd-1335.html and information about the Wang case is at http://www.justice.gov/opa/pr/2013/December/13-enrd-1284.html.

Another recent "Operation Crash" success is *United States v. Michael Slattery, Jr.*, (E.D.N.Y.). On January 10, 2014, Slattery (an Irish national) was sentenced to serve 14 months' incarceration, followed by three years' supervised release. Slattery also will pay a $10,000 fine and forfeit $50,000 of proceeds from his illegal trade in rhinoceros horns. In 2010, Slattery traveled from England to Texas to acquire black rhinoceros horns. Mr. Slattery admitted to illegal trafficking throughout the United States, and is alleged to belong to an organized criminal group engaged in rhino horn trafficking. This organized criminal element speaks to the scope,

scale, and lawlessness of this problem. More information about this case is available at:
http://www.justice.gov/opa/pr/2013/November/13-enrd-1181.html.

"Operation Crash" cases, like the Wang case above, may also include charges related to
the illegal smuggling and sale of elephant ivory. The Division has seen success in other elephant
ivory cases. In *United States v. Tania Siyam* (N.D. Ohio), Siyam, a Canadian citizen, was
sentenced in August 2008 to five years' incarceration and a $100,000 fine for illegally smuggling
ivory from Cameroon into the United States. Siyam originally operated art import and export
businesses in Montréal (Canada) and Cameroon that were fronts for smuggling products from
endangered and protected wildlife species, including raw elephant ivory. The two ivory
shipments to Ohio included parts from at least 21 African elephants.

Another ivory case, *United States v. Kemo Sylla, et al.* (E.D.N.Y.), concerned the illegal
importation of ivory over a two-year period through New York's JFK Airport. The ivory was
disguised as African handicrafts and wooden instruments. The six defendants pleaded guilty to
Lacey Act violations and received sentences ranging from one year of probation to 14 months'
incarceration. A number of the defendants also were ordered to pay fines to the Lacey Act
Reward Fund. More information about this case is available at:
www.justice.gov/usao/nye/pr/2011/2011mar03.html.

Still other prosecutions involve the illegal import or export of endangered species. For
instance, in *United States v. Nathaniel Swanson* (W.D. Wash.), three defendants were recently
sentenced (following guilty pleas) to incarceration (ranging from 5 months to one year),
supervised release and an order to pay $28,583 in restitution for conspiracy to smuggle various
turtle and reptile species from the United States to Hong Kong, including Eastern box turtles,
North American wood turtles, and ornate box turtles. One of the defendants also illegally
imported several protected turtle species from Hong Kong, including black-breasted leaf turtles,
Chinese striped-necked turtles, big-headed turtles, fly river turtles, and an Arakan forest turtle.
The Arakan forest turtle is critically endangered, having once been presumed extinct. The illegal
trafficking spanned approximately four years. More information about this case is available at
http://www.justice.gov/usao/waw/press/2014/January/swanson.html.

B.   Working in the International Sphere: Training and Capacity Building

For many years, prosecutors and other Division attorneys have worked closely with our
foreign government partners to build their capacity to develop and effectively enforce their
wildlife trafficking laws, better enabling them to combat local poaching and the attendant illegal
wildlife trade. The Division's training efforts have focused on the legal, investigative, and
prosecution aspects of enforcing against wildlife crime. We seek to help our partners craft strong
laws, strengthen their investigation and evidence gathering capabilities, and improve their
judicial and prosecutorial effectiveness. Our experience has shown that such training develops
more effective partners to investigate and prosecute transnational environmental crimes,
increases our ability to enforce U.S. criminal statutes that have extraterritorial dimensions while
also helping law enforcement officials in the U.S. and other countries meet their enforcement
obligations under international environmental and free trade agreements. These training

initiatives also foster positive relationships with prosecutors in other countries in a way that better enables us to share information and assist in prosecuting transnational crimes.

We often conduct our international training in close collaboration with the Department of State and other federal agencies, such as the Department of the Interior and the U.S. Forest Service. Capacity building may be conducted bilaterally (in the United States or a partner nation) or in multilateral fora, and our programs may span a range of environmental crimes. In particular, I would like to highlight the Division's extensive participation in training and general support for foreign investigators, prosecutors and judges through the various Wildlife Enforcement Networks ("WENs"). These include the Association of Southeast Asian Nations WEN ("ASEAN-WEN"), South Asia WEN, and Central American WEN, as well as the launch of WENs in Central, Southern, and the Horn of Africa. We have conducted workshops in multiple countries in these regions that involved dozens of agencies from the host countries, and typically have included hundreds of participants representing government, the judiciary, industry and civil society. The workshops are a mix of direct course instruction on legal and wildlife trafficking enforcement issues, including presentations by U.S. environmental prosecutors, and an opportunity for representatives from the different countries to exchange views on the issues they face. Thus, these sessions are both a valuable training opportunity as well as an opportunity to develop a law enforcement network in that region.

The Division has also been involved in numerous international training efforts focused on enhancing prosecutions brought under the Lacey Act, the United States' oldest plant and wildlife protection statute. With the amendment of the Lacey Act in 2008 to protect a broader range of plants and plant products, much of our recent capacity building work has focused on the trade in illegally harvested and traded timber and timber products, an illegal trade conservatively estimated at a value of $10-$15 billion worldwide. The National Strategy recognizes that wildlife trafficking is facilitated and exacerbated by the illegal harvest and trade in plants and trees, which destroys needed habitat and opens access to previously remote populations of highly endangered wildlife.

ENRD has conducted numerous training sessions abroad on investigating and prosecuting illegal logging cases in Indonesia, Brazil, Peru, Honduras, and Russia with financial support from the State Department and Agency for International Development. The training agenda may vary somewhat from country-to-country, but is typically done in close collaboration with the foreign government and local prosecutors. Such collaboration benefits and strengthens criminal law enforcement in both countries.

The Division conducts further international capacity building in the area of illegal wildlife trafficking through its participation in INTERPOL (specifically the Wildlife Crime Working Group, Environmental Crime Committee, and Fisheries Crime Working Group) as well as the International Law Enforcement Academy (with programs for eastern European and southeast Asian law enforcement officials).

C.   The National Strategy to Combat Wildlife Trafficking

The Department is proud of its record of achievement in this area, but the National Strategy is a reminder that more must be done. The National Strategy calls for a "whole of government" approach and increased federal coordination to address three key priorities: (1) using the full range of mechanisms to enhance domestic and international law enforcement to curb the illegal flow of wildlife; (2) reducing the demand for illegally traded wildlife; and (3) using the United States' influence to mobilize global support for the fight against wildlife trafficking. The National Strategy resulted from the analysis, contributions, and expertise of 17 federal agencies, led by the Task Force co-chairs, the United States Departments of State, Interior and Justice. The National Strategy also benefitted from the contributions of the Advisory Council on Wildlife Trafficking established by the July 1, 2013, Executive Order. Coming from outside the government, the Advisory Council brought experience and diverse skills to the process and represented the many different communities that will have to be engaged as partners to tackle this problem.

The result is a robust, coordinated and far-reaching National Strategy that addresses the multiple dimensions of this growing crisis, and the Department is proud to have played a major role in developing the National Strategy. Naturally, the Department's role in that process, and our expected role in implementing it, is focused on that first priority -- domestic and global law enforcement. Strong enforcement is critical to stopping those who kill and traffic in these animals, whether on land or in the oceans. And, as is described above, the Department of Justice has for many years aggressively pursued and prosecuted those engaged in the illegal wildlife trade. We have also worked vigorously to train and support partner countries in their efforts to stanch this terrible crime.

As we look toward the implementation of the National Strategy, those enforcement and capacity building efforts will be enhanced and intensified. Department prosecutors will continue to target traffickers and their networks, investigate and prosecute them, bring down their leaders, and disrupt the illicit finance that flows to and from these syndicates. We will focus on making illegal wildlife trafficking much less profitable by using the tools of fines and penalties, seizure and forfeiture, and payment of restitution to those victimized by illegal trafficking. The Department will also strengthen our coordination of enforcement efforts, looking for ways to improve the way we work with our federal partner agencies (including through the improved sharing of intelligence), as well as state and tribal authorities.

We also look forward to working with the Congress to strengthen existing laws and adopt new legislation to improve the tools available to address this challenge. The law should place wildlife trafficking on an equal footing with other serious crimes, for example, by recognizing wildlife trafficking as a predicate crime for money laundering. We can also more effectively fight the scourge of wildlife trafficking if Congress passes legislation that allows for investing funds generated through wildlife trafficking prosecutions into conservation efforts or to combating wildlife trafficking, as well as to ensure adequate authority to forfeit all proceeds of wildlife trafficking.

Looking globally, the Department will continue to help source, transit and demand countries to build their capacity to take action against illegal wildlife traffickers. Given the transnational dimension of this problem, we will continue our support and training of existing Wildlife Enforcement Networks and look to support additional regional WENs, where appropriate. And more directly, recognizing that illegal wildlife trafficking is a growing area of transnational organized crime, we will support and engage in enforcement initiatives together with the enforcement authorities of other nations. Such efforts, of course, just as those domestically, will target the assets and seek to impede the financial capacity of international wildlife traffickers.

IV. CONCLUSION

In closing, I would like to assure the Committee that ENRD remains fully committed to doing its part.

Mr. Chairman, I would be pleased to answer your questions and those of Members of the Committee.

Chairman ROYCE. Thank you very much. If I could go to Mr. Ashe first with the observation, Director Ashe, that Fish and Wildlife has began to do with the Embassies exactly what we have had the DEA or FBI do in the past, which is to say you are starting to station. I guess, in Thailand you have done this.

We are trying in sub-Saharan Africa. I guess it is in the paperwork to get one of your—one of your agents in the Embassy there. I wonder—and I think it is in Tanzania that you are focused on that.

Is there anything Congress could do to help expedite that and get that in place, get those agents on the ground in the Embassies?

Mr. ASHE. I think, as you said, with the help of the State Department and USAID we have had—we have had success. We will have our first law enforcement agent stationed in Bangkok later this month.

We are working with the State Department. Our goal through the end of this year is to have two agents in Africa, two agents in Asia and one agent in Latin America, and we—and I think that the most important thing for Congress, obviously, is to provide the financial support for that.

We will—we did receive an increase in the most recent appropriations bill. We would hope to receive additional funding in the coming year to provide further support for this effort and encouragement, of course, Mr. Chairman.

Chairman ROYCE. When we checked in on Tanzania, what was the hold-up at State on that? Do you know offhand or——

Mr. ASHE. I do not know the particular hold-up.

Chairman ROYCE. If there is anything we can do to expedite that just——

Mr. ASHE. Tanzania is—actually, what we are trying to do is station an expert in Tanzania that is not law enforcement. At this point, Tanzania has not requested law enforcement assistance so a little bit different situation in Tanzania.

Chairman ROYCE. Likewise, most of us have been out there to talk to the head of state and to the legislature. I know Karen Bass makes frequent trips to that area.

So if there is anything we can do with their legislature or their executive branch to elicit that request, especially given what is being looted out of—trafficked out of Tanzania, we would be happy to do that.

I am curious on another subject. Since the Attorney General and the Secretary of State consult with the Treasury Secretary on the designation process, there is existing authority to go after transnational criminal organizations that could be used here because the Treasury Department has the ability to sanction property, sanction assets of transnational criminal organizations.

So how would the Department of Justice request to Congress to place wildlife trafficking as a predicate crime for money laundering, bolster the effort in—to attack the financing aspect of this if you feel that is important, and if you do is it possible from the panel here that we might get legislative language to do exactly what DOJ suggests here? Can you get me that draft language?

Mr. DREHER. Mr. Chairman, we welcome your interest in this and we would be happy to work very closely with the committee to try to develop language. The National Strategy does ask for help from Congress.

We are seeking to have the same law enforcement tools that we have available to us to combat other very serious forms of transnational crime, and for wildlife trafficking some of those tools are more limited than we would benefit from including, in particular, making wildlife trafficking a predicate offense for money laundering charges.

We would also seek help in making—getting clarification of our authority for asset forfeiture in cases where the predicate offenses were wildlife trafficking. We really want to try to take the profit out of this crime.

But, Mr. Chairman, we would be happy to work with the committee and as closely as we can.

Chairman ROYCE. That language would be very helpful and very welcomed, I think, by the committee and we would work that out and move it quickly.

Local community-based conservation was the other aspect of this that I wanted to ask you about. When I was chair of the Africa Subcommittee one of the trips we took with Secretary Colin Powell was to Central Africa.

We spent time there with Michael Fay, National Geographic explorer in residence, who explained to us the critical importance of supporting on-the-ground local actors who are on the front lines of this fight, who have a stake in the fight, and realizing the impact that local community engagement could bring to conservation and we went forward and authored the Congo Basin Forest Partnership Act.

Now, with our wildlife trafficking crisis, what unique role does community-based conservation play and what is their potential here for reducing wildlife poaching and how could we better work with these local community groups who now have a stake all right in—you know, through their sustainable development practices of, basically, monitoring the population there—the elephant populations and so forth.

How might we be able to work with those community-based organizations? Director Ashe.

Mr. ASHE. Again, I think working collaboratively is the key to that and that is this—the power in this all of government approach.

Certainly, we have—we have had within the Fish and Wildlife Service, within our international affairs program we have for decades now focused on building capacity within range state nations and I think that that is what we have to do and we have to build local incentive for the conservation of these species, and the State Department has been a great partner in that effort.

Again, it is resource limited. We have great NGO partners, many of whom will be stepping up their efforts as well.

But I think what you reference, Mr. Chairman, is the key that we have to—we have to work at the community level. We have to build capacity, law enforcement, economic development capacity related to these issues.

We can't do that—any one of us cannot do that alone. We have to—we have to do that together. We have to have many, many more resources to get the job done.

Chairman ROYCE. The last issue I was going to ask your collective support for is an aspect that wasn't mentioned in the strategy and that is the role of the Defense Department.

Many of the park rangers in these African countries don't have the capacity to fend off poachers because they are outgunned and many of these African countries depend on their militaries, frankly. They use the military there to protect the wildlife and to protect the borders.

So the DoD has a long relationship with some of these armed forces, leveraging those relationships by having them provide the training to these military forces, or advising them could be very helpful in combating poaching.

But I can tell you there has been a lot of—there has been a lot of push back from the DoD in the past when I have talked to them about this or we have floated this issue.

I think it would be very helpful if the three of you would sort of expand this strategy to include that component because if we are serious about preparing these park rangers they are going to need a little bit more help than just what we are talking about here.

You are going to have to bump it up, and I think you are going to find that the DoD has provided technical assistance to African armed forces. It would just be changing the attitudes of DoD to get them to understand that this is part of subverting transnational crime and some of these terrorist groups and others who are benefitting out of this by cooperating.

What do you think about that, Director Ashe—whether the three of you think that is possible.

Mr. ASHE. I think, again, the opportunity for increased intelligence capacity, increased information sharing, training on the ground can certainly be enhanced by the involvement of the U.S. Defense Department.

I would say, Mr. Chairman, I think one of the tragedies in all of this is, you know, if you will recall about 18 months ago we lost—we, the collective we—lost a park ranger at Mount Rainier National Park in an unfortunate incident and caused a moment of, certainly, within the entire Department of the Interior and I think within the nation as a whole, a moment of grief.

Well, we see, you know, that one national park—Virunga National Park in the Congo—over the last decade they have lost 100 rangers trying to protect these animals.

So we need better—we need to better equip and train them and we need to provide mechanisms of support for their families because when those rangers are lost that is a family's income, a family that is essentially put at risk. And so we need better tools to deal with that aspect of this.

Chairman ROYCE. Well, what I am trying to get you to focus on is if the DoD is going to provide technical assistance to African armed forces, if you expand this to the park rangers and get them that capacity. Right now, they are outgunned.

So I think you need to be—you need to convey that and see if you can't get us a little bit—if we get the administration to support that, frankly, that would be very helpful because we just went through a round here late last year on this. So that is, I guess, what I am asking you to do.

Dr. Jones, if you could convey that and——

Ms. JONES. Yes.

Chairman ROYCE [continuing]. Try to—the three of you rally around that I think it would be helpful.

Ms. JONES. If I may, Chairman, one of the strengths—I think it was—is this on now? One of the strengths of the approach that we have in the task force is that DoD is a member of this task force and we have been in discussions with DoD and with AFRICOM and we——

Chairman ROYCE. Right. Right.

Ms. JONES [continuing]. And we will continue those and I——

Chairman ROYCE. And there is no mention of the strategy or role for the Defense Department in this document. That is why I am pushing you. I am saying we got push back last year.

I am just saying if they are outgunned, you know, you have got some people out there that can give them that capacity and the intel and sort of level the playing field and we want you to really push on that.

My time has expired and I am going to go to Karen Bass. Thank you very much.

Ms. BASS. I just want to follow up on that because I know in the discussions that I have had with AFRICOM while traveling and with DoD there just didn't seem to be—just didn't seem to be a real high priority. So I would definitely appreciate that message being sent.

Along with that, you know, I also think of equipment that we might be able to be helpful with. I know in one country we talked about the use of drones.

In Gabon, for example, that wouldn't work because of the rain forage—rain forests. But in other countries, you know, it might be a very appropriate use.

I wanted to ask some questions, following up from the conversation that we were having before the hearing started, about the U.S. in terms of the—you mentioned before how most of the ivory is passing through but then there are also consumers in the U.S.

I, prior to this, didn't really view our country as a problem. I thought it was more overseas, and so I wanted to know your opinion about what we should do here in terms of current law, increasing penalties, deterrents, et cetera.

What are your ideas that we should do here?

Mr. ASHE. Thank you, Congresswoman Bass.

I think the first step is to end commercial trade in the United States. So as you mentioned, you know, in Los Angeles you can visit probably dozens of antique stores. You can do that here in Washington, DC, New York City, Seattle. Any major U.S. city you can go into an antique store and see items like this for sale.

It is very difficult from a law enforcement perspective to tell the difference and tell that this is an antique—it is 100 years old— something else is not. And so we need to end the trade and so that is one step we can take.

Ms. BASS. Well, you know, actually the stores that I was mentioning are not antique stores.

Mr. ASHE. Right. They are just bazaars. You can go to the Dulles bazaar, the monthly bazaar here at Dulles Airport and there will be probably a dozen, you know, stalls where people are selling ivory products and so——

Ms. BASS. It is kind of hard to say if you have 100 items that are exactly the same that they are antiques.

Mr. ASHE. And so what we have—what we have found is the legal trade in ivory has become a smokescreen effectively for a burgeoning new trade because the value of these products is so high and has escalated so dramatically.

So we need to take that step and it is not just important from the standpoint of ending the trade. It is important from the standpoint of establishing U.S. leadership on this issue.

So the next big step is to use diplomacy on the global level to reduce demand and that is—long term that is the most important ingredient and the U.S. has to be able to speak from a position of leadership and I believe our ban on ivory trade in the U.S. sets an example for the world as our crush of ivory did back in November. It allows us a position of leadership in the world and a voice of leadership.

Ms. BASS. Any other comments? Thank you.

Ms. JONES. I think that Director Ashe's point about the leadership is one that we have a real opportunity to move forward on now. Just a short while ago, the Prime Minister of Vietnam went out to all of his ministries and said you need to now pay more attention to wildlife trafficking, very similar to what we did with the—President Obama did with his Executive order, and Secretary Kerry had raised this with the Prime Minister during a visit and talked about this issue.

So I think that our ability to sort of have a full court press in all of our diplomatic engagements and being very credible about what we are doing at home and also talking about how we can work together will begin to bring down both the supply and demand.

But our challenge now is to maintain momentum and I think with this strategy and the implementation plan that will come from it we will be able to do that.

Ms. BASS. You know what? In thinking about my trip to Botswana and how they were able to—actually, the same villagers that understood that this was part of their economic development prior had been participating in poaching.

And I am just wondering if there is, you know, some role that the U.S. might play in either technical assistance, education in other communities around the continent where you have people who are actually participating—you know, the residents in the community that lives nearby because they are desperate because of the poverty.

They are seeing it from a very shortsighted perspective and if that might be a role that the U.S. could play is to go around and provide that technical assistance to show how this could actually improve your development and not view it so shortsightedly.

Ms. JONES. Well, I had the opportunity to travel to Tanzania where I visited some of the USAID programs that try to do that.

Ms. BASS. Okay.

Ms. JONES. They have programs called Wildlife Management Areas where a community actually looks at the economics of being able to have tourism in their area and it is a jointly-owned process.

I sat in a room where they looked at income from tourists coming in and there was a real sense of what the value of the wildlife and their whole environment was to that community. And so there is a long history of doing that and I think there are more examples of that spreading in different countries through different activities of USAID.

Connecting that then to national policies which have more protection and also have better national policies will, I think, make a big difference from local all the way up to the national.

Ms. BASS. And I know I am out of time, Mr. Chairman. Just quickly, what about the African Union? Do you think the African Union is aggressively taking this issue on? Are we working with them?

Ms. JONES. Yes. We are—we are working with them. We have raised it with them and we continue to raise it with them. I would think that it is something that they have responded to.

My former boss, Under Secretary Hormats, raised it with the leader of the African Union and we will continue to do that.

I think our approach has been, from a diplomatic standpoint, to work at this bilaterally, regionally, through international organizations, through every channel we can. And so that is the approach we are going to keep.

Ms. BASS. Okay. Thank you. Thank you, Mr. Chairman.

Chairman ROYCE. Mr. Rohrabacher of California.

Mr. ROHRABACHER. Thank you very much, Mr. Chairman.

Couple of—just look at some specific suggestions, and Mr. Attorney General or Assistant Attorney General, would you—I think you mentioned asset forfeiture and could we have—today if the assets are seized from these people who are breaking the law and are poaching and are being destructive of this natural resource, does that then go into the fund for preserving them and enforcing the law or does the asset forfeiture just go into a general law enforcement fund?

Mr. DREHER. There is some opportunity to direct funds that are seized or assets that are seized into law enforcement funds that can have some benefit for us. The Endangered Species Act, for example, has a fund program that lets us use it for some limited purposes.

There isn't—there isn't an ability to really direct the assets that are seized directly to law enforcement in a larger way. It is a very limited opportunity, and in many cases when we seize assets under other statutes, when we, for example are charging crimes involving smuggling, you know, the assets will go directly to the Treasury and not to law enforcement activity.

Mr. ROHRABACHER. Mr. Chairman, I would suggest that perhaps a source of revenue for this effort would be that we direct the assets that are seized from people who are breaking the law by murdering these species that that be directed specifically to that fight.

That might increase the capabilities of those who are enforcing the law.

In terms of technology, is there—we have incredible intelligence technology today. We can zero in, and do these countries that are trying to oversee large areas where you have poachers actively murdering these elephants and rhinoceroses—do they have the capability—do they have technological capability that would be affordable to them to get that job done? Whichever—Mr. Ashe.

Mr. ASHE. I would say across the board, Congressman, no. I mean, as Chairman Royce indicated in his opening statement that what we have seen, because of the escalation in value and demand for these products the—you know, criminal networks have upped their game.

And we used to deal with poaching, which is—you know, much like we deal with poaching in the United States, it was opportunistic. It was locally driven by local economies.

We now see organized syndicated trafficking networks and they have—they are very sophisticated. They have access to technology and arms and equipment that our—that our colleagues in these range states do not have.

Mr. ROHRABACHER. So in terms of overseeing a large animal reserve in Africa, we have people who are at a great disadvantage because they do not have what perhaps an infantry squad in Afghanistan would have——

Mr. ASHE. Correct.

Mr. ROHRABACHER [continuing]. Available to them. All right.

That is—we have a lot of—Mr. Chairman, we have a lot of excess military equipment that—left over from these adventures in the Gulf that might be available to these people at a very low cost because we have it there.

And who would—Secretary Jones, what countries would you give gold medals to and what countries would you put on the dirty guys list?

Ms. JONES. That is a very good question. What I have been seeing in my travels is that the governments—many of the governments are trying to do the right things and much of the poaching and the activity is coming from groups that cross borders.

I think that a country like Tanzania is trying very hard to do the right things. I think that South Africa is trying. I think Kenya is trying. I know that there has been an effort with the legislators in Kenya to look at policies.

So in terms of engagement and our discussions, we are seeing a lot of leaning into the right policy directions. It is the implementation question.

Mr. ROHRABACHER. I am going to put you on the spot because what happens quite often—I always ask the question is what are your most highest priority for budget issues, which are lowest priority, and everybody is always willing to give their high priorities but they are never willing to tell us the low priority because they know that that is where we will cut. In terms of the question I just asked——

Mr. CONNOLLY. Mr. Rohrabacher, my lowest priority in the budget is defunding Obamacare.

45

Mr. ROHRABACHER. Thank you. Madame Secretary, you gave us some good countries.

Do you have any bad boy countries that we should put on our list of people who are not doing the adequate job and perhaps intentionally not, maybe through corruption or whatever? I notice you didn't mention Zimbabwe or any other country like that.

Ms. JONES. No, I don't have—I mean, honestly, I don't have a country I would put on that list and it is—from my perspective, it is not a budget issue. I mean——

Mr. ROHRABACHER. Oh, no. I am not talking about budget. I am just saying who you are telling us we got to watch out for these guys because they are not—they are not only not doing a good job, they may be in cahoots with the bad guys, versus you gave us a few lists there of people that deserve a gold medal, and which one deserve the, you know, bad recommendation?

Ms. JONES. I think—I don't think I can answer that question because I am—seriously, you know, I would turn to Director Ashe to maybe say what he is seeing on the ground.

But from a policy perspective, what I am hearing is that the governments are trying to take the right actions. So I would turn to Dr. Ashe and maybe he is going to say on the ground.

Mr. ASHE. Congressman, I guess I would say that the most important thing right now is we have the opportunity to learn that. I think what we are finding is that these—because of the value of these products they are finding the path of least resistance and often times that is not the range state. The range state is tak- ing——

Mr. ROHRABACHER. I see. Yes.

Mr. ASHE. So I think the important thing is for us to learn the answer to your question. I think right now we don't know that. It looks like the bad guy might be Zimbabwe or it might be Congo or it might be—but really, they may be doing everything they can do within their power. So I think we need to learn that.

Mr. ROHRABACHER. Well, I know if we are talking about fish and sharks that the Chinese like to have their shark fin soup and they are destroying—I—we used to when I was a kid—I am a surfer and all that—I used to spend a lot of time and I—frankly, surfers and sharks don't get along. But I like to eat shark. I mean, I—we used to barbecue it.

But the fact is that the Chinese, with their consumption patterns are destroying sharks—the whole shark population around the world and that is an issue of concern and I would—Mr. Chairman, I would think that whether it is China or elsewhere, the consumers of these products—those governments need to be brought to task as well. Thank you very much.

Chairman ROYCE. And take shark fin soup off the menu.

Let us go to Gerry Connolly of Virginia.

Mr. CONNOLLY. Thank you, Mr. Chairman, and I would like to pick up on Mr. Rohrabacher's question because what he is getting at is the word efficacy.

It is not—it seems to me, if we care about this subject it is not satisfactory that somebody is bending into the right policies—doing the best it can.

The question is, is it effective? Are we losing this battle or are we winning it, and what are the metrics that get us to winning? And Mr. Rohrabacher's question has to do with bench marking. What are the best practices and, bottom line, are they working? Otherwise, they are not best practices.

So, Dr. Jones, let me reframe the question. As we look for models where there are clear metrics, where there is the commitment of the government, there are the resources in place and in fact we are seeing trafficking go down and the organized traffickers moving on somewhere else because it is just too hard there, what would you cite? Where would you cite?

Ms. JONES. Thank you, Congressman.

I think that question gets at the two parts of this problem—the supply and demand—because we have been talking about both market countries and range states. And, certainly, the U.S. and China are two of the biggest markets for these products.

And shark fin soup was also mentioned and there have been campaigns that have shown that there has been an effect in reducing the demand for that by outreach.

So we have been increasingly engaged with the Chinese to work on market demand because the reason these prices are so high is because people will put out the money for this.

So I would say that we do need benchmarks. We are at the turning point.

I can't—I can't tell you exactly how much we have done with China to reduce demand of ivory right now but I think what we need to do as we move into this implementation plan is look at how the outreach going to affect demand, how are we going to increase seizures, how many more rangers are we going to have on the ground and how many national policies do we have.

So it is from the ground up to the policy that we have to have benchmarks and we will just have the strategy out and we are going to get to that with the implementation plan, but to make the point that it is both pieces of this.

It is the supply, demand and transit and so we have to have benchmarks for each piece of that and that is what we are working toward.

Mr. CONNOLLY. Dr. Jones, I appreciate that commitment but this problem is not a new problem. One could infer from what you just said that we are pretty far behind the curve here in—and we are not—we don't even have an implementation strategy to set benchmarks or metrics? We are just getting around to that?

Ms. JONES. Well, we are just getting to an implementation plan based on this recent strategy.

Mr. CONNOLLY. Is there a single country of origin, hold in abeyance China or the United States as consumer countries, but is there a single country of origin you can point to where substantial progress has been achieved, where poaching is down and animal populations are either stabilized or, in fact, growing?

Mr. ASHE. Mr. Connolly, I would—I would suggest Namibia.

Mr. CONNOLLY. Namibia.

Mr. ASHE. Namibia is an excellent example of a country that has an exceptional program and record. There are 5,000 black rhinoceroses left in the world. Eighteen hundred of those are in Namibia.

Mr. CONNOLLY. We might not—we might not want to bring too much attention to that.

Mr. ASHE. Right. That is right. And so we—what we owe those countries is support. So, for instance, I mean, Namibia right now is, you know, going through a process of allowing the harvest of a black rhino.

They can—they have a—they have a quota of up to five per year. They have never filled their entire quota and right now it is very—it has become very controversial because they are going to allow the harvest of a single black rhino. But we owe them support——

Mr. CONNOLLY. Yeah.

Mr. ASHE [continuing]. Because they are the gold standard. And so I would suggest Namibia and so that we can expand that example throughout Africa.

Mr. CONNOLLY. And I think you have just put your foot—your finger on something that I think is really important. Look, we have got to be bottom line focused here, including the State Department. Are we making progress or are we falling behind?

You can have the best strategy, best policy, the best aspirations in the world and still lose the game, and where we find a good actor who is not only trying to do the right thing but actually making progress, I agree with you—then let us get behind them big time to show others the reward system that faces them if they start to put the resources in to try to, you know, fight back against the poachers and the traffickers because I have to say, Mr. Chairman, I am alarmed at what I am hearing in this hearing.

Not lack of effort, not lack of commitment but we are losing this game. We are not—we are not making progress and we are up against actually something far more organized, far better financed, far more violent and dangerous on the ground than most of the local governments or even military can, frankly, handle.

And we are going to have to think through our strategy here and make it a lot more robust if we are going to begin to turn the tide. Otherwise, we are going to lose this battle.

Thank you, Mr. Chairman.

Chairman ROYCE. Mr. Connolly, I think you are right. On a lot of fronts we are—we are losing. In Namibia, we are winning or Namibia, I should say, is winning and part of that is because they have a community-based local conservation program of the first rank there and it is something of a template.

Mr. CONNOLLY. Yes.

Chairman ROYCE. And if that can be expanded then on other fronts I think the tide can be turned.

Mr. CONNOLLY. And Mr. Chairman, just to underscore—just to underscore what you said, because you are putting your finger exact, we have got to look at benchmarks.

We have got to look at best practices and try to encourage them elsewhere. Otherwise, we can have a lot of international agreements and strategies and goals and policies but meanwhile we are losing—we are losing the game.

Thank you, Mr. Chairman.

Chairman ROYCE. Thank you.

Randy Weber.

Mr. WEBER. Thank you, Mr. Chairman.

In reading through this report it brings up a whole lot of questions and I guess it does get the bench marking and what my friend, Mr. Connolly, was saying, trying to get a benchmark and trying to make progress.

So I have got some questions. In our report—and this is not from you all's testimony but I do want you all to answer the questions if you can—we talk about eyewitness accounts from the Lord's Resistance Army, LRA, which talks about some of the abductees, for example, Joseph Kony has ordered his fighters to get elephant tusks and they are going to terrorist groups.

Are we building a database of the terrorist groups that are involved in this kind of trafficking?

Ms. JONES. Thank you for the question.

We are closely following all of the activities and the different kind of illicit groups that are involved. So there are terrorist groups. There are militia groups. There are some just rogue military and then you have that collection tied into organized and syndicated crime.

And so yes, we are certainly doing more to have information on some of these issues and to also work with our partners to get more information. So yes, we are trying to move forward on that.

Mr. WEBER. Okay. Are we communicating those terrorist groups to our military forces, those who are responsible for the war on terror?

Ms. JONES. We are sharing our information with the appropriate players.

Mr. WEBER. Okay. And have they taken any action that you know of against these groups based on the information that you have sent them, Dr. Jones?

Ms. JONES. I can't speak to that at this time here.

Mr. WEBER. You do know that this is not the appropriate setting?

Ms. JONES. Yes.

Mr. WEBER. Okay. Then we will talk offline. And then keeping in line with that questioning, of those terrorist groups that we are identifying with the database, are we rating and ranking them in what order are the most—the most active and second most active?

Ms. JONES. It is difficult to talk about all the details at this—in this setting. There is a lot of information we are trying to gather and also share that with partners and other players and we are continuing to sort of raise the importance of this issue as how it ties into all of these networks and their activities.

Mr. WEBER. Okay. Because we are talking about funding but—in the war on terror. You know, once we have identified these groups and you even—in our report it talks about there are certain—seems to be certain routes that they use in smuggling across the different countries.

You talk about them traversing country lines, state lines, borders. Have we identified those routes? Are we, you know, staking out those routes?

Ms. JONES. We are beginning to track those routes and we are beginning to sort of use that information in how we respond and share it with partners in sort of the coordinated operations that I was mentioning in my testimony, these different sharing of information between all of the countries involved in Africa and Asia to understand those routes.

So I think we are in the process of getting more information on how all of these different illicit activities are coming around this activity because this is just about—this is about money and so we are tracking the money.

We have to follow the money and that is one of the things we are really working on from both——

Mr. WEBER. Okay. That is a great segue to my next question about the money because we have instituted a rewards program. How successful has that been? Is it paying out? Are we—how successful has that been?

Ms. JONES. Well, we have just started that as the legislation expanded that reward system to include wildlife crime. So it is just in November that we have announced the first reward and I haven't heard—I haven't gotten any feedback on that yet. But I can get more and get back to you.

Mr. WEBER. Okay. And then you mentioned Namibia, I think, as being a success story. On the scale of countries—on the scale of the amount of trafficking, where do they fall? Are they number two? Are they number 22?

Mr. ASHE. I would put them at the top of the scale.

Mr. WEBER. Well, now, that is in success.

Mr. ASHE. Right.

Mr. WEBER. But in terms of volume.

Mr. ASHE. Volume—well, they have little trade and so from a— from the standpoint of risk they are low on the scale. So they have a very effective management and customs control regime so——

Mr. WEBER. Okay. And then last question—I am running out of time—so, I mean, I don't mean to disrespect them or the assessment that they are a success story but if they have little traffic— if they are a small country and they didn't have a whole lot to fight then it would have been easier for them to be able to fight that.

Are we rating countries' governments on how they respond to this problem—some of them are cooperating, some are not? Are we rating those governments?

Mr. ASHE. We are—we have not to date. I think that is the point. I can go back to a statement Mr. Connolly made that, you know, this has been going on for a long time. I guess I would say it has not.

I mean, what we have seen in the last 24 months is a dramatic escalation, 7,000 percent rise in the value of rhinoceros horn. And so what we have seen in just the last 24 months is that these things have become so lucrative that these syndicated networks have rushed in.

And so we are just learning about that and so the routes of trade, for instance, what—our traditional approach to dealing with wildlife poaching is you go after the poachers. You get the poachers.

And so what we now need to do is we need to let these things move so that we can discover their routes of trade and who is making the money and where they are. And so we are—we are just beginning and the questions you are asking are the right questions and we need to—we need to do that.

We need to identify which countries are the risk, both the source countries, the transit countries and then the demand countries—where are the highest risks and how can we stack and attack those.

Chairman ROYCE. Maybe—Mr. Weber, maybe I could answer some of that because in the case of al-Shabaab, to go right to your question, in September 2013 al-Shabaab, of course, attacked the Westgate Shopping Mall in Nairobi.

Sixty-seven people were killed there and 200 people were wounded, and shortly after that attack the Kenya President Kenyatta identified illegal trade in ivory as a source of funding for the terrorist group.

And President Kenyatta made it very clear—I think I—I think this was in the Wall Street Journal where I read this—where he said al-Shabaab acts as a facilitator and broker, you know, in ivory.

One of the reports we have shown that al-Shabaab gets up to 40 percent of the funds necessary for its operating expenses through the ivory trade. The calculation of the quantity on the black market is up to 600,000 monthly.

So when a terrorist organization like that is looking for hard currency and they are demonstrably involved in this activity and the consequences of this is that they are able to sustain an operation in which they, you know, create casualties to this extent, and as the President said this cannot be curtailed without an offensive against overseas buyers and he said we need a global plan to end a business that endangers our wildlife and bankrolls a tax on our people in Kenya.

That would be one example, but also from 2012 we had the situation with the Janjaweed and many of us are monitoring what they have done not just in Darfur, of course, and in Chad but in the Central African Republic.

But in—on March 2012 the Janjaweed perpetrated one of the worst elephant slaughters in recent history anyway, riding over 600 miles from Sudan all the way to the national park in Cameroon. There, they slaughtered more than 300 elephants—more than 300 elephants.

That is the just the attack on Cameroon. They also attacked Chad. They also attacked several other countries. They went through Kenya on an attack. So you have these terrorist organizations that aren't just a threat to wildlife.

I mean, they are carrying out ethnic cleansing, frankly, or carrying out military operations against those who they feel are their enemies.

But one of their sources of hard currency is what they are doing in the rhino and ivory elephant trade.

Mr. WEBER. Thank you.

Chairman ROYCE. And so that is why I want to give you the specifics on that. But we go now to Grace Meng of New York.

Ms. MENG. Thank you, Mr. Chairman and Ranking Member, for holding this important hearing.

As you know, China in recent months publicly destroyed large quantities of ivory, and sort of a two-part question. The first part is I wanted to get your take on whether you think there has been enough action behind this great symbolism, and second, we talked about shark finning before.

I have been a very small part of a national effort to eliminate the consumption of shark finning. We have been successful as of last year in New York State, not only via law enforcement methods but also in terms of education and increasing cultural awareness.

And I also would like to get your take on the cultural elements affecting the demand side here in the U.S. or abroad and what are some strategies we can use to reach out to communities where demand for ivory is high.

Ms. JONES. Thank you.

The Chinese did destroy about—I think it was six tons maybe of ivory recently and we took that as a very good sign but is a sign—it is a symbolic sign of moving away from sort of a national support of this kind of trade.

But more substantively, we have been working closely with the Chinese and we have been seeing a strong interest on their part to partner with us on a number of ways of looking at this.

So they have been very active, as I mentioned, in this international operation to look at all of the different points along the trade route, those COBRA operations where COBRA II recently, I think, had something like an increase of 400 arrests and 350 seizures and China was a partner in that activity.

Now, that is in a multilateral setting but we are also seeing—we have engaged the Chinese through the strategic and economic dialogue, which is one of our main bilateral engagements, to discuss issues with them.

And last year for the first time we discussed wildlife trafficking in this forum for our strategic relationship and our economic dialogue which show the importance of it and it was a very engaged discussion and we have been having very good follow-up on this.

So there is engagement and there is interest. There is also—we have been working with the China-U.S. joint liaison group on law enforcement because there are all these different pieces of the problem that have to get attention.

So, clearly, China realizes that it is a large market for these products. We are also a large market so we have been trying to assume a leadership together on this and engage in every way that we can.

We have a lot of work to do but I do think that there has been some progress and I personally have been involved in the discussions. We also see it in our relationship on illegal logging, which is related to this issue.

Now, the point about changing demand, we have been talking about that because there is a cultural issue. There is a younger generation coming up in our country and around the world that is very conservation minded and we are working with the Chinese about messaging how do you get this out. That was a very important part of the whole shark fin campaign.

So I think there is a lot we can do and we are getting, as I said, a very positive response.

Mr. ASHE. Ms. Meng, I would say one thing about the ivory crush and the elimination of confiscated stockpiles is that we have seen encouraging results initially at the—at last year's conference of the parties for the Convention on International Trade in Endangered Species.

There was agreement that all parties to the convention, 179 member nations, should report on their stockpiles and that is due by the end of February. And so by the end of February, we will have a sense of what are nations carrying in terms of stockpiles.

The U.S. stockpile, which we destroyed in November, was about six tons. A country like China would have many times that, and so having that information we will then be able to put that in context because it is not just the symbolism. It is the risk that that—those stockpiles represent because they have to be secured.

In the U.S. our stockpiles are very secure. In other European nations they would be very secure but in many of the range and demand countries the security of those stockpiles is an issue.

Ms. MENG. Thank you. I yield back.

Chairman ROYCE. Thank you.

We will go to Ted Yoho of Florida.

Mr. YOHO. Thank you, Mr. Chairman. Appreciate you being here today, and it just—I never cease to be amazed at the stupidity, ignorance and brutality and greed of my fellow man on something like this.

I want to build on Ms. Meng's questioning on the cultural elements. You are seeing that change in the Asian countries where the big demand is. We can only hope that we do more of that.

I assume you have videos of these animals slaughtered, the remnants of that, and I assume this goes through a regular business transaction.

You have the supply side, which is the animal, and then you have the facilitator, the poacher, then the facilitator, the broker and eventually the buyer.

What is the poacher on an average—is there an average figure that they receive out of this and is there an economic incentive we can say don't do it—we will give you the money?

Ms. JONES. I can sort of give you an estimate for one that I remember when we were discussing this with the Kenyans. I think the amount that the poacher was getting was like five times the annual salary of a ranger. It was some inordinate factor.

But that may be off. I mean, Dan may have a better number on that.

Mr. ASHE. Like, in terms of the value—the end value of the product they are getting very little. But in terms of the comparison to their—what they could otherwise make they are making very much.

Mr. YOHO. So they are making thousands?

Mr. ASHE. By equivalent, yes.

Mr. YOHO. Yes.

Mr. ASHE. And so I think that is the issue that the chairman mentioned, the community-based approaches to these challenges. It is very important that the people see a value in an elephant tusk that is beyond the immediate harvest because that represents a dead elephant. That represents a dead rhinoceros. So that is a one-time harvest.

Mr. YOHO. Right. And that also represents a lifestyle for somebody for 2 or 3 years probably in those countries, right?

Mr. ASHE. Correct.

Mr. YOHO. Yes. And they are looking at their family or lifestyle. The demand side, again, I just, through education, you know, it just—it is mind boggling that somebody thinks that, you know, they are going to get a hangover and they are going to crush up some rhino horns and make a powder and, you know, instead of just educating them a better way to deal with their problems instead of getting rid of our resources.

And if you look at the life span of a rhinoceros, it is, what, 45 to 60 years and, you know, sexual maturity of the female is, I think, 6 to 8 years of age and the males 10 to 12 and they have got about a year and a half gestation period.

Is anybody looking at, and I don't even know if I want to go here, but animal husbandry to raise them and then harvest the ivory? Because you were saying in Namibia that they allow for the harvesting of a male.

I mean, are they using a tranquilizer gun or is it it is killed— shoot to kill and then have your picture taken with it? I mean, are they looking at using tranquilizers and then removing the antler or the horn versus killing the animal?

Mr. ASHE. There have been a lot of—of course, elephants you can't remove the tusk. Any kind of ranching or farming of elephants is difficult because they are slowly reproducing long-lived animals.

Mr. YOHO. They sure are.

Mr. ASHE. Rhinoceros, they are—you can remove the horn from a rhinoceros. There has been some experimentation with doing that but they grow back and at the value of these horns if you cut the horn off, you know, low even that little bit is extremely valuable. And so there have been attempts to—at what we would call traditional management approaches to this and because of the value of the products they are—they have been largely unsuccessful.

That doesn't mean we can't try in the future. The case I mentioned in Namibia is a sport harvest so that would be—that is a, you know, post-reproductive male that is essentially outcompeting reproductive males.

They need to take it out of the population for good management purposes. The individual who would harvest that has, you know, purchased the—you know, the privilege to do that for, I think, close to $300,000. All of that money would go back into management. That is why Namibia has such an exemplary program.

Mr. YOHO. Let me get your opinion on doing the ivory crush and breaking the supply side. Is that going to increase the value of them, obviously, and is that going to create more demand and a more black market? I guess you can't get any much more of a black market.

Mr. ASHE. The material that we crushed was confiscated—is contraband.

Mr. YOHO. Right.

Mr. ASHE. So it would never go into trade. So destroying it would have no——

Mr. YOHO. But it decreases the supply side so the demand or the value is going to go up on the stuff they can get, right?

Mr. ASHE. No, because it would have never been in trade anyway.

Mr. YOHO. But I am talking about future procurement of the horns.

Mr. ASHE. Presumably, but if you end the demand—if you end the trade and you end the demand then that is the way, I think, we have to deal with it. We have——

Mr. YOHO. I agree. I mean, that would be the best way and just get people off of this stuff. I just find it horrendous that people are doing this in the 21st century. Thank you.

Chairman ROYCE. Thank you, Mr. Yoho.

We go now to Mr. Matt Salmon of Arizona.

Mr. SALMON. Thanks a lot, Mr. Chairman. I think it goes without saying that we all support the idea of protecting and preserving and cultivating endangered species all around the globe, particularly elephants and rhinoceroses.

This hearing is really helpful as we look toward the best models of how to access and address—excuse me, address this program globally. Mr. Ashe and Dreher, as you are working on new regulations on the domestic sale of ivory—I am talking about ivory that is already legal and here, not the future stuff—I think it is important that we avoid the trap of intended consequences.

Specifically, I would like to urge you to adopt rules that do not harm U.S. collectors—I mean, people that already have it within the family.

I am particularly concerned about families that might have a family heirloom currently that is ivory, which could be, you know, a gun handle or a knife handle or a statue which has been passed down from generation to generation with little regard of paperwork sometimes.

And so I am hoping that as we develop the rules we don't get a situation where we are essentially taking family heirlooms and making them worthless. And so while I completely support going forward and making sure that, you know, that folks that are acting in an illegal way that we prosecute them to the nth degree of the law and that we make sure that, you know, that we do this for the future.

But how can we balance in rule making to make sure that people that have had legal ivory in their homes for years—from years and years and years aren't hurt by the, you know, law of unintended consequences?

Mr. ASHE. It is a difficult proposition although I would say unequivocally that people who have a family heirloom that has been passed from generation to generation can continue to pass that heirloom. They can own it. They can possess it. They can move it.

Mr. SALMON. They can't sell it, though.

Mr. ASHE. They cannot sell it.

Mr. SALMON. And that, to me—I mean, it renders the thing basically valueless.

Mr. ASHE. If it is a family heirloom it strikes me that the value is in the generational value of the product. The challenge for us is that these products are—it is very difficult to judge the authenticity of them because of the value of them and the relatively low penalties associated with trafficking in them that the risk is low, the value is high and so legal trade is a significant smokescreen for effective law enforcement.

Mr. SALMON. I understand that it might be difficult. But what I am saying is not all—I mean, I might have an heirloom. What if I have a Picasso that is left to me but maybe my folks leave it to me and we come on economic hard times and we decide, you know, I need to sell that Picasso because of the value of the product.

I am saying something that has been in the family for a long, long time is there a way to do rule making so that we prosecute the bad guys that are trying to exploit, you know, new ivory, exactly what you are trying to accomplish.

Your goal is not to punish people that have owned legal ivory for the last 100 years. Your goal is to make sure that for the future that we don't have bad actors and further, you know, dealing with causing extinction or, you know, a dwindling of those resources.

So is there a way to develop the rule so that people that have had legal ivory don't get caught in the cross hairs?

Mr. ASHE. I think there is a statutory exemption in the Endangered Species Act for antiques over 100 years of age and but what we will have to do is ask for rigorous documentation.

Now, if you own something that is extraordinarily valuable like a Picasso or a, you know, a Steinway you are going to have that documentation because you will be able to show a trail of transaction over many periods because they are extremely valuable.

And so I think that people will be able to document that for things that are—that have extraordinary value.

Mr. SALMON. What if I—what if I owned a firearm that had ivory grips on it and perfectly legal, but I sold the firearm? Am I going to be in the cross hairs of the government because I am—you know, I am selling something that I have owned for several years but I have decided I want to sell it?

Mr. ASHE. Well, I guess I would—from the standpoint of the U.S. Fish and Wildlife Service, our priority for law enforcement is syndicated commercial-scale trafficking.

Mr. SALMON. Okay.

Mr. ASHE. We are not looking for the average American, although it would, under our proposed ban, if that firearm is not an antique then it would be illegal for you to sell it and the—and you would need to be aware of that.

And so I think that is—we do—it is our opinion that we do need to end the legal commerce in ivory and we need to do that at some point in time.

Mr. SALMON. Okay. Thanks, Mr. Chairman.

Chairman ROYCE. Mr. Ted Poe—Judge Poe of Texas.

Mr. POE. Thank you, Mr. Chairman. Thank you for being here.

I am very concerned, like a lot of folks are, about this actual disappearance of some of the world's animals because of these outlaws that are killing them and selling them for money. It is all about that filthy lucre, money, and it involves a lot of bad guys—terrorists, criminal gangs, you know, solo thieves and bandits.

But it is all about the money, and I am really concerned that they may be actually eliminating species, that they are so successful that they are not breeding enough of these animals to catch up with the robbers of their lives.

Lacey Act—I want to talk about that. Hypothetical question and, really, I am looking for some answers on what we can do, Congress, to go nail these people. Maybe that is not polite language, certainly not diplomatic language.

But anyway, we got a company—let us use the hypothetical—operating in Africa, and they are a conservation company and they trade in endangered animals. They violate the Lacey law.

If they are an American company they are subject to the Lacey law in the United States. Is that correct? American company, they are violating the Lacey law, operating in some African country and they could be prosecuted under the Lacey law. Is that correct?

Mr. DREHER. I think the predicate offense in a Lacey Act violation is putting into commerce or importing into the United States an article that is taken in violation of foreign law.

Mr. POE. Oh, yes. That is assumed.

Mr. DREHER. So they would have to be bringing it into the United States. Yes.

Mr. POE. They are bringing in—they are bringing it to America.

Mr. DREHER. And if they are doing that in violation of the host country's wildlife laws, yes, that would be a Lacey Act violation.

Mr. POE. Go after them. Nail them. But you got a foreign country doing exactly the same thing in the fact that they recruit. They are in violation of the Lacey law in other areas.

But let us say they advertise in the United States. They recruit hunters to go to their little game ranch wherever it is in Africa but they are notorious for operating and trading in illegal, you know, ivory or whatever it is.

But they still are able to get access to American hunters and advertising because the Lacey law doesn't apply to them. Is that—is that correct?

Mr. DREHER. Again, I think unless the American participants are bringing in to the United States——

Mr. POE. They are not doing that. They are not bringing it in.

Mr. DREHER. They are not bringing back trophies?

Mr. POE. No. But you got this corporation—foreign corporation operating, doing the same thing only they are operating in another country.

The only thing they do in the United States is recruit hunters to go and they—you know, hunters go and, you know, don't bring the trophies back—illegal trophies back in the country.

My real question is how can we get the Lacey law or some type of action to go after these independent foreign corporations that are doing this and really competing with the, you know, good corporations of the United States that have vast amounts of land that they conserve, doing the right thing, but they compete with these guys that are involved in the trade?

I don't know that I framed the question very well. What can we do to go after those folks I guess is really my question. What can we do legally—legislatively? Ideas—I am open to ideas, Dr. Jones.

Ms. JONES. Yes. There are a couple of things that come to mind, Congressman. I think you raise a very good dimension of this. One is the typical diplomatic route. We work with these countries to show them how the Lacey Act works and sort of try to encourage them to have laws just like it. So we do try to do that.

The second thing is in trade agreements, that we have environmental provisions that elevate this and try to ensure that countries involved in trade relations are dealing with issues like this and following international agreements like CITES and that is part of the requirement in the trade agreement.

And so we do have environmental sections of our trade agreements and we are in the process of trying to put these into some of the new agreements that are under negotiation.

Mr. POE. Can't we at least prohibit those companies—we know about their—what they are doing in another country. We can't reach them because they are a foreign company. Can we prevent them, since they are doing this activity, from at least advertising and recruiting in the United States?

Mr. ASHE. If they are—I think, as Dr. Jones mentioned, we have other international instruments like the Convention on International Trade and Endangered Species and if their activities are undermining the implementation of those other international instruments then we can bring an action.

We can sanction those countries under the Pelly Act so we have—we do have mechanisms to ensure that international instruments are being effectively implemented. They are not being undermined. And so perhaps we should look at the Pelly Act. But I would applaud you, Congressman, for your reference to the Lacey Act.

It is the workhorse of national and international wildlife law enforcement and I would just, you know, say to the committee tomorrow there is a hearing before another committee of this House of Representatives where some significant actions are being considered that will weaken our ability to enforce the Lacey Act.

And so we need effective voices to not just maintain the Lacey Act but strengthen the Lacey Act as a means of enforcement.

Mr. POE. All right. Thank you, Mr. Chairman.

Chairman ROYCE. Yes. Thank you, Judge Poe.

And, again, we thank our three witnesses here. We especially want to thank also the NGO community that are really integral to, frankly, the partnership that has got to be put together here to bring the amount of tension necessary to elevate this issue before it is too late, as I indicated in my opening statement, before we reach the point where these species have been slaughtered to the point of extinction.

So thank you all for your efforts here, and we will be back in touch because we do need that draft language, your assistance on that front, and thank you again to our witnesses.

We stand adjourned.

[Whereupon, at 11:47 a.m., the committee was adjourned.]

A P P E N D I X

MATERIAL SUBMITTED FOR THE RECORD

FULL COMMITTEE HEARING NOTICE
COMMITTEE ON FOREIGN AFFAIRS
U.S. HOUSE OF REPRESENTATIVES
WASHINGTON, DC 20515-6128

Edward R. Royce (R-CA), Chairman

February 26, 2014

TO: MEMBERS OF THE COMMITTEE ON FOREIGN AFFAIRS

You are respectfully requested to attend an OPEN hearing of the Committee on Foreign Affairs, to be held in Room 2172 of the Rayburn House Office Building (and available live on the Committee website at http://www.ForeignAffairs.house.gov):

DATE: Wednesday, February 26, 2014

TIME: 10:00 a.m.

SUBJECT: International Wildlife Trafficking Threats to Conservation and National Security

WITNESSES: The Honorable Kerri-Ann Jones
Assistant Secretary
Bureau of Oceans and International Environmental and Scientific Affairs
U.S. Department of State

The Honorable Daniel M. Ashe
Director
U.S. Fish and Wildlife Service
U.S. Department of the Interior

Mr. Robert G. Dreher
Acting Assistant Attorney General
Environment and Natural Resources Division
U.S. Department of Justice

By Direction of the Chairman

COMMITTEE ON FOREIGN AFFAIRS
MINUTES OF FULL COMMITTEE HEARING

Day __Wednesday__ Date____ __02/26/14__ ____ Room_____ __2172_____

Starting Time __10:11 A.M.__ Ending Time __11:47 A.M.__

Recesses [__0__] (____to ____) (____to ____) (____to ____) (____to ____) (____to ____) (____to ____)

Presiding Member(s)

Rep. Edward R. Royce, Chairman

Check all of the following that apply:

Open Session ☑
Executive (closed) Session ☐
Televised ☑

Electronically Recorded (taped) ☑
Stenographic Record ☑

TITLE OF HEARING:

International Wildlife Trafficking Threats to Conservation and National Security

COMMITTEE MEMBERS PRESENT:

See Attendance Sheet.

NON-COMMITTEE MEMBERS PRESENT:

None.

HEARING WITNESSES: Same as meeting notice attached? Yes ☑ No ☐
(If "no", please list below and include title, agency, department, or organization.)

STATEMENTS FOR THE RECORD: *(List any statements submitted for the record.)*

SFR - Engel
IFR - Royce
QFR - Royce
QFR - Duncan

TIME SCHEDULED TO RECONVENE _____
or
TIME ADJOURNED __11:47 A.M.__

Jean Marter, Director of Committee Operations

HOUSE COMMITTEE ON FOREIGN AFFAIRS

FULL COMMITTEE HEARING

PRESENT	MEMBER
X	Edward R. Royce, CA
	Christopher H. Smith, NJ
	Ileana Ros-Lehtinen, FL
X	Dana Rohrabacher, CA
	Steve Chabot, OH
	Joe Wilson, SC
	Michael T. McCaul, TX
X	Ted Poe, TX
X	Matt Salmon, AZ
	Tom Marino, PA
	Jeff Duncan, SC
	Adam Kinzinger, IL
X	Mo Brooks, AL
X	Tom Cotton, AR
	Paul Cook, CA
	George Holding, NC
X	Randy K. Weber, Sr., TX
	Scott Perry, PA
	Steve Stockman, TX
	Ron DeSantis, FL
	Doug Collins, GA
	Mark Meadows, NC
X	Ted S. Yoho, FL
X	Luke Messer, IN

PRESENT	MEMBER
X	Eliot L. Engel, NY
	Eni F.H. Faleomavaega, AS
	Brad Sherman, CA
	Gregory W. Meeks, NY
	Albio Sires, NJ
X	Gerald E. Connolly, VA
	Theodore E. Deutch, FL
	Brian Higgins, NY
X	Karen Bass, CA
	William Keating, MA
X	David Cicilline, RI
	Alan Grayson, FL
	Juan Vargas, CA
	Bradley S. Schneider, IL
	Joseph P. Kennedy III, MA
	Ami Bera, CA
	Alan S. Lowenthal, CA
X	Grace Meng, NY
	Lois Frankel, FL
	Tulsi Gabbard, HI
	Joaquin Castro, TX

National Rifle Association Questions
"International Wildlife Trafficking Threats to Conservation and National Security"
February 26, 2014
U.S. House of Representatives Committee on Foreign Affairs

1. Director Ashe, can you outline in detail how, under the proposal, a current, legal owner of ivory more than 100 years old would document their antiques? What if there is no existing documentation as to its pre-ban status?

   FOLLOW UP: If the owner is able to meet the requirements outlined for antique ivory, will it be legal to transfer the ivory, and what are any new requirements for doing so?

2. Director Ashe, how would a trade ban on legally owned pre-1990 ivory in the U.S., including such items as ivory inlaid firearms and pianos with ivory keys, reduce poaching and the illegal trade in ivory?

   FOLLOW UP: Isn't this just another burdensome requirement for law-abiding gun owners in the U.S.?

3. Acting Assistant Attorney General Dreher, if the ban on legally owned ivory goes into effect, will the Administration pay restitution to lawful gun owners whose ivory collections become valueless because they lack the proper documentation or their items are less than 100 years old?

4. Director Ashe, how would restricting elephant sport-hunted trophies to two per hunter per year help to reduce poaching and the illegal trade in ivory?

5. Director Ashe, it is my understanding members of the hunting community, who are experts on ivory trade, asked to sit on the Wildlife Trafficking Task Force to offer their expertise, but were rebuffed by the Administration. Is this true, and if not, who on the Wildlife Trafficking Task Force represents the hunting NGO community?

   FOLLOW UP IF NOBODY NAMED: Why wasn't a member of the hunting NGO community given a seat on the Council?

National Rifle Association Statement
"International Wildlife Trafficking Threats to Conservation and National Security"
February 26, 2014
U.S. House of Representatives Committee on Foreign Affairs

Mr. Chairman, the National Rifle Association (NRA) appreciates the opportunity to submit a statement for the record on the subject of international wildlife trafficking. The subject of the hearing was prompted by the release of the Administrations' National Strategy for Combating Wildlife Trafficking (National Strategy). The National Strategy has a direct bearing on American hunters legally hunting in Africa, as well as a prospective impact on law abiding gun owners, dealers, and manufacturers who legally own or sell firearms and firearm accessories containing ivory components in the United States. Thus, the NRA has a vested interest in the controls the Administration intends to implement under the National Strategy.

Illegal trade in wildlife, as well as poaching for meat and products, such as horns and tusks, not only takes its toll on the health and sustainability of wildlife populations, but it also undermines the billions of dollars that have been invested in the restoration and conservation of wildlife species by millions of American hunters. While the objectives of the National Strategy are laudable, the NRA has concerns with its implementation.

The National Strategy sets three priorities: strengthening domestic and global enforcement; reducing demand for illegally traded wildlife at home and abroad; and strengthening partnerships with international partners, local communities, NGOs, private industry and others to combat illegal wildlife poaching and trade. Of concern is that an offer of partnership to address poaching and illegal trade was extended by the hunting community and rebuffed by this Administration. The Advisory Council on Wildlife Trafficking provided significant input to the Presidential Task Force which was created to oversee the development of the National Strategy. Yet, not one qualified individual from the hunting community with expertise in African elephant conservation was invited to serve on or consult with the Advisory Council.

Of equal concern is the National Strategy announcement that it will extend the present ivory trade ban to ivory lawfully imported prior to 1990. The NRA does not yet know the impact the extension of the ban on ivory legally traded in the United States will have on firearm owners, dealers and manufacturers who may have antique firearms, specially made firearms, or firearm accessories containing ivory components. If an owner does not have provenance, such as with firearms that have been handed down in the family, the firearm could now be made valueless by such a ban. It is our belief extending such a ban will not discourage poaching and illegal trade, and will not provide the tools to better target wildlife criminals. It is nothing more than a burdensome restriction on law abiding gun owners who legally own these firearms and firearm accessories.

Two weeks ago the US Fish and Wildlife Service, as part of a proposed rulemaking, announced it intends to limit sport-hunting of African elephants that an individual can import to two per hunter per year. The NRA is concerned about this ill-advised and scientifically unsupportable restriction on sustainable hunting because it is not known how many hunters will be affected, as well as the hundreds of thousands of dollars to local communities and wildlife conservation that will be forfeited. What makes this announcement particularly unproductive is that it is hunters' dollars in license fees and other expenditures that support locally-based conservation in Africa, and enable local African communities to encourage sustainable wildlife as part of their economic well being. There is no evidence hunters in this country are contributing to the decline of elephant populations in Africa.

While the case may be made for stepped up measures to address the serious and urgent conservation and security threat posed by illegal trade in wildlife, the NRA is concerned unreasonable, unworkable, and unbeneficial bans and restrictions will get swept up in the zeal to stop poaching and illegal trade. The National Strategy is calling for certain actions that make no contribution to the reduction of illegal ivory trade and poaching. The National Strategy does nothing more than impose restrictions on legal hunting and law-abiding gun owners by rendering their legally owned, pre-ban ivory firearms and accessories containing ivory components valueless by prohibiting their trade. Further, such actions will result in losing a net-gain in African wildlife conservation.

 Each of the actions the Administration intends to take needs to be scrutinized through the lens of its National Strategy priority of reducing demand for illegally traded wildlife at home and abroad, and that the actions make a measurable reduction in wildlife poaching.

The NRA appreciates the opportunity to submit this statement for the record and stands ready to provide further comments and recommendations.

Statement for the Record
Submitted by the Honorable Eliot L Engel

Chairman Royce, thank you for holding this timely hearing on an increasingly urgent issue – the illegal wildlife trade.

On February 11, the administration released a comprehensive strategy to combat global wildlife trafficking. That same week, at a meeting in London, 46 countries agreed to take new steps to eradicate the supply and demand for illegal fauna and flora.

This destructive and morally repugnant trade includes high-profile items like elephant ivory, rhino horns, and tiger parts, but also numerous other plants and animals, including exotic birds, timber and flowers.

The soaring demand for these products as gifts, medical cures, and pets is having a devastating impact on animal populations around the world.

For example, a report by the Bronx-based Wildlife Conservation Society and a number of other organizations found that elephants in Central Africa have declined by almost two-thirds since 2002, largely as a result of poaching. In total, more than 47,000 African elephants were killed in 2011 and 2012.

It's a terrible tragedy that rampant wildlife poaching is driving iconic animal populations toward extinction. But there's also a national security dimension to this growing crisis.

Illicit wildlife trafficking has become one of the world's most lucrative international criminal activities, generating an estimated $10 to $20 billion every year. This is surpassed only by drug, human and arms trafficking as a source of illegal revenue.

The proceeds from "blood ivory" are increasingly used by insurgents and terrorist groups to purchase weapons and support other nefarious activities, which contribute to instability in Central and East Africa.

These illicit financial flows also contribute to the corruption of public officials, which undercuts U.S. efforts to improve rule of law and governance.

In Africa, natural resources are the foundation on which many countries intend to build their economic sectors and graduate from aid to self-reliance. However, the increasingly violent and rampant pilfering of these resources is a significant hindrance to the continent's future economic growth and financial independence.

In order to stem the continued rise of these destructive forces, we need to address the illegal wildlife trade on both the supply and demand sides. In "source" countries, we must bolster the capabilities of forest rangers and other law enforcement. But we must also tackle the large market in the United States and the growing demand for wildlife products in Asia.

To that end, the President's strategy would ban the U.S. commercial ivory and rhino horn trade by closing loopholes in existing law. On the international front, it would set up public information campaigns with partner counties to help consumers make informed decisions about the consequences of purchasing wildlife products.

We should also continue efforts to strengthen domestic laws and support law enforcement efforts. Last month, the Justice Department and the Fish and Wildlife Service worked together to successfully convict a rhino horn trafficker in my home state of New York as part of a nationwide operation called "Crash".

Internationally, I support the President's efforts to strengthen regional wildlife enforcement networks, which improve coordination among law enforcement personnel from various nations. And I encourage greater cooperation between those networks and the existing North American Wildlife Enforcement Group, of which the Fish and Wildlife Service is a part.

As we examine the wildlife trade and the administration's strategy, I'd like to hear from the panel on how soon the various parts of the strategy will be implemented. I'd also be interested to know if Congress should consider any changes to current law to enhance our efforts abroad.

The President's national strategy and the recent London declaration are important signs that the United States and the international community are prepared to do more to stem the wildlife trade.

But as we commemorate World Wildlife Day this coming Monday, words must be followed by action.

Thank you Mr. Chairman and I look forward to hearing from the panel on those actions.

Questions for the Record
Submitted by Chairman Ed Royce
To the Honorable Daniel M. Ashe

<u>Question 1:</u>

Executive Order 3648 established a "Presidential Task Force on Wildlife Trafficking," co-chaired by the secretaries of State and Interior as well as the Attorney General. A major responsibility for the Task force was producing a "National Strategy for Combating Wildlife Trafficking." Now that the National Strategy is completed, what are the next steps for the Task Force?

<u>Answer</u>

[RESPONSE NOT RECEIVED AT TIME OF PRINTING]

<u>Question 2:</u>

The national strategy called for supporting community-based wildlife conservation. The strategy explains that "local communities are essential partners on the ground and can be a powerful force in support of wildlife conservation and a frontline defense against poaching." Please describe these community-based approaches to natural resources management in Africa. What form do they take? How is the U.S. supporting these efforts? How do community-scouting and ranger programs work? And, what is their potential for reducing wildlife poaching?

<u>Answer</u>

[RESPONSE NOT RECEIVED AT TIME OF PRINTING]

<u>Question 3:</u>

The national strategy announced administrative changes to elephant ivory trade regulations, including revoking exemption that allows African elephant ivory to be traded in any way that would otherwise be prohibited by the Endangered Species Act. When do you suspect this new regulatory rule to be issued? Will the rule be issued on emergency basis allowing for expedited consideration? Will the FWS follow statutory rulemaking requirements, including but not limited to publishing a notice of proposed rulemaking in the Federal Register and the consideration of public comments. In what ways are these changes likely to reduce the global illegal trade in ivory? What threat does trade in antique grandfathered ivory pose? Under what circumstances would you see a need for legislative solutions to implement a complete moratorium on all commercial trade in ivory in the United States?

<u>Answer</u>

[RESPONSE NOT RECEIVED AT TIME OF PRINTING]

Question 4:

The most developed part of the National Strategy was the closure of the "loopholes" that made the U.S. ban on elephant ivory largely ineffective, primary of which was eliminating broad administrative exception to the 1989 African Elephant Conservation Act moratorium. What are the key gaps that the regulations you announced will be closing? How confident are you that the steps outlined by your agency will effectively close down U.S. markets to illegal ivory? In particular, are there additional federal authorities needed to close intra-state trade in ivory and rhino horn?

Answer

[RESPONSE NOT RECEIVED AT TIME OF PRINTING]

Question 5:

Some sportsmen and hunting organizations have expressed concerns of the possible adverse efforts the commercial ban on ivory trading may have on legal hunting activities, although they have taken no formal position since rules have yet to be proposed. Could legal hunting activities be jeopardized by the ivory ban? In what ways did the Task Force solicit feedback from sportsmen?

Answer

[RESPONSE NOT RECEIVED AT TIME OF PRINTING]

Question 6:

A number of governments have recently destroyed large stock piles of seized ivory. The U.S., China, Hong Kong, and France, are among the few that have particapted in these "ivory crushes." What is the purpose of an ivory crush? How do they help in combating wildlife trafficking? Some analysts have questioned the effectiveness of the ivory crushes from an economic perspective, since destroying large amount of ivory reduces the supply thus raising the value of the ivory that remains on the market as well as the incentive to poach. Does the Administration share these concerns?

Answer

[RESPONSE NOT RECEIVED AT TIME OF PRINTING]

Question 7:

The National Strategy specifically calls for the U.S. Postal Service (USPS) to continue to print and sell the Save Vanishing Species Stamp, which existing law already allows them to do, so that it can provide critical funding to the MSCF. Is the U.S. Postal Service still offering the stamp to costumers? Was the Postal Service involved in developing the National Strategy?

Have any conversations taken place with the leadership at the USPS to advise them of their role in implementing the strategy by issuing this stamp?

Answer

|RESPONSE NOT RECEIVED AT TIME OF PRINTING|

Question 8:

Can you outline in detail how, under the proposal, a current, legal owner of ivory more than 100 years old would document their antiques? What if there is no existing documentation as to its pre-ban status? If the owner is able to meet the requirements outlined for antique ivory, will it be legal to transfer the ivory, and what are any new requirements for doing so?

Answer

[RESPONSE NOT RECEIVED AT TIME OF PRINTING]

Question 9:

The ban on all ivory trade in the US will render pre-ban legally owned ivory as of value only as family heirlooms. Would this make legal owners of pre-ban ivory, such as ivory art collections, jewelry, ivory inlaid firearms, ivory-key pianos, rendered worthless monetarily?

Answer

|RESPONSE NOT RECEIVED AT TIME OF PRINTING|

Questions for the Record
Submitted by the Honorable Jeff Duncan
To Ms. Kerri-Ann Jones, Mr. Daniel M. Ashe, and Mr. Robert G.Dreher

Some sportsmen and hunting organizations have expressed concerns about possible adverse efforts the commercial ban on ivory trading in President Obama's July 1, 2013 Executive Order Combating Wildlife Trafficking may have on legal hunting activities. America's hunters are the first line of defense in protecting wildlife from poaching, and trophy hunting conserves wildlife and provides needed revenue to many countries. Regarding the ivory ban, the focus of this effort should be on the conservation of live elephants, not putting unrealistic burdens on families for passing down heirlooms that already have ivory in them.

Question 1

How is someone supposed to determine whether or not their possessions contain ivory that qualifies as an "antique" for purposes of this proposed action? How is this going to be enforced?

Answer

[RESPONSE NOT RECEIVED AT TIME OF PRINTING]

Question 2

What is the rationale for limiting legal sport hunted elephants to two per year per hunter?

Answer

[RESPONSE NOT RECEIVED AT TIME OF PRINTING]

Question 3

If there are agreed upon quotas for sport hunted elephants from qualifying African countries, why is there a need to arbitrarily limit how many a given hunter might take in a year?

Answer

[RESPONSE NOT RECEIVED AT TIME OF PRINTING]

Question 4

In what ways did the Task Force solicit feedback from sportsmen on this proposed policy change?

Answer

[RESPONSE NOT RECEIVED AT TIME OF PRINTING]